Consulting 101

101 Tips for Success in Consulting

2nd Edition

By Lew Sauder

Order Lew's other books today:

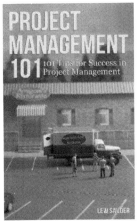

Project Management 101: 101 Tips for Success in Project Management

The Reluctant Mentor: How Baby Boomers and Millenials Can Mentor Each Other in the Modern Workplace

Library of Congress catalog number: 2013917722

Consulting 101: 101 Tips for Success in Consulting 2nd Edition/ by Lew Sauder.

ISBN 978-0-9830266-4-8

Additional copies of this book can be ordered from the publisher, CreateSpace (www.Createspace.com), or from your favorite online bookstore.

For more information go to:
www.LewSauder.com
Lew@LewSauder.com

Consulting 101

Consulting 101

Dedicated to my family:
Emily, Sam, Holly, and Heather

"Success is not the key to happiness. Happiness is the key to success. If you love what you are doing, you will be successful."

Albert Schweitzer

Acknowledgements:

The stories and advice in this book are the direct result of my association with many gifted and intelligent people. Over the years I have had the privilege to work with incredible individuals who taught me effective consulting techniques. I would like to thank the following people for their leadership and mentoring throughout my career: Michael Curran, my first consulting manager, for giving me my start and helping me to develop the tools and confidence to work in a consulting environment; Richard Gibbs Vandercook for his friendship, guidance, and leadership. His war chest of great stories and even better advice are present throughout this book; Robert Simplot, president of RCG Information Technology, for teaching me that strong management and great leadership can be attained without sacrificing being a decent and down to earth person.

Thanks to Jeff Porter for partnering with me in the first edition for the audio book and our weekly podcasts. I look forward to our regular conversations for both enjoyment and growth. Your advice and belief in me have made a big difference on the writing side of my life. I look forward to our future collaborations.

I am grateful for the detailed editing efforts from Stephanie S. Diamond for her detailed editing skills. Her grammatical knowledge and attention to detail combined to make this a much better final product. You can contact Stephanie for her services at:
https://www.facebook.com/StephanieSmithDiamo nd

Consulting 101

Thank you to Jennifer Wells for your patience and outstanding photography and cover design.

Thank you to my wife, Heather, for her many hours of proofreading and advice in the creation of this book and her many years of support throughout my career.

And finally, thanks to my late mother, Helen Sauder, for her unshakable confidence and support throughout my life and to my late father, Lee Sauder, for teaching me that anything worth doing is worth doing right. You were right, Dad.

Table of Contents

Preface

Early in my consulting career the firm that I worked for asked me to drive three and a half hours from Chicago to Indianapolis to meet with a client. We were to discuss development of an imaging system. I had just recently been trained on the imaging package and had written only a few applications for one other client.

I walked into a conference room with about a half-dozen people in it and I was introduced as an "expert" in imaging systems. They said I was there to help them develop an imaging application to interface with their Accounts Payable system.

The inflated introduction was a bit intimidating--I knew even less about AP systems than imaging systems. It stroked my ego enough to try my best to live up to the label. I reached back into my memories of my training and my lone client experience. I started asking questions about their work flow. I took them through the who, what, where, and when of their payment processing to understand their current process. I drew a diagram on the white board to regurgitate what they had just told me in a pictorial form and used another color to insert scanning stations to input invoices and purchase orders to the imaging system. Next I added terminals at key points to represent points in the process where users could view the images on-screen. It was a simple future-state design and they were thrilled with what the "expert" had done in one short meeting.

Consulting 101

Most people dream of being an expert at something. Having expertise in a specific area lends a combination of prestige, credibility, and acceptance to one's branding. To be an expert in a specific area of business translates into being successful and in demand. Much like a homeowner might hire a plumber or building contractor for a home project, businesses turn to consultants as experts to provide advice and services for which they either don't have the expertise or the staffing to perform themselves.

Having a depth of knowledge in a subject matter, however, does not necessarily translate into success in the consulting world. In most cases, a successful consultant is a professional with a combination of many skills that provide value to their clients.

Ego enhancement is not a reason to pursue a career in consulting. Consulting is a demanding and competitive career that often requires long hours, hard work, and the ability to deal with difficult people. It is also a rewarding endeavor that pays above average and provides experience and opportunities that are not available in many other occupations.

In addition to some business or technical know-how, consulting requires a multitude of additional skills. You need to have the ability to think on your feet and utilize diplomacy for resolving conflict. A consultant must also balance being customer centered while keeping the firm's interests at hand.

Throughout my career, as I moved into management positions in consulting, I've worked with many new employees. They were either "newbies" out of college or experienced workers who had never worked in consulting. I found it frustrating at times. Although they had the business and technical skills to do assigned tasks, they lacked the softer skills that are so important to successful consulting. There was often a lack of awareness that the client was the paying customer and should be treated differently than a peer. They treated the project in a transactional approach rather than establishing a relationship with the client to improve the chances of acquiring additional work. In meetings there were times where the consultants exposed some of the firm's "dirty laundry" to the client.

I'd meet with my peers over lunch and we would share stories of how our consultants weren't provided proper training in basic blocking and tackling skills. Those skills are critical because they help teach the professional behavior that every reputable consultant needs. That is why this book was created--to provide a primer to anyone who is considering joining a consulting firm, starting their own firm, or simply working as an independent consultant. Most of the tips include case studies of real-world examples of mistakes I've witnessed over the years (and some that I've made myself).

As I wrote this book, I started with a much larger list and pared it down to what I thought were the most important issues to address. Even then, I found a lot of the advice to be basic--almost common sense. However, if it's common sense, then why did I see these tips violated nearly every day? Much of the advice in this book is guidance in professionalism that can--and should--be used by anyone joining the business world. In most companies, this is nice-to-have advice. In consulting, it is imperative business behavior for success. In order to establish credibility and legitimacy with a paying client, there are certain guidelines that must be followed.

One final note: I was once at a week-long firm outing in which spouses were invited. One evening a group of folks ended up in the hotel's bar. One younger consultant who was a bit over-served was using foul language and cursing at every opportunity. Thankfully there were no clients present, but the wife of the firm's president was in the group.

The next morning at breakfast, a senior manager who had been with them in the bar pulled the young consultant aside and advised him about how inappropriate his language was in the presence of the president's wife. The hung-over consultant apologized, saying it wouldn't happen again and thanked the manager for his advice. As they headed for their table, the president's wife came up to him and said, "There you are you son of a bitch, how are you feeling this morning?"

The moral of the story here is that not all advice applies in all situations. There are 101 pieces of advice in this book and not every one will fit for every client in every circumstance. At some point, your own good judgment should take over once you get acclimated to the firm you join and your assigned client.

The focus of this book is on larger solution-based firms and their structures, although much of the advice applies to consultants at any level in any tier of consulting.

What are consultants used for?
Business organizations use consultants for many purposes depending on their needs.

To bring in the experts. Suppose a software company has identified a reduction in demand for their product over the past twelve months. Their marketing strategy has not changed significantly over that period. They are wondering if there has been a major shift in public opinion of their product or possibly in their market's needs. They decide to bring in a marketing consulting firm to perform some market studies. This should help them determine what is causing the shift in demand and to develop a marketing plan to reverse the trend. Most companies already have marketing divisions to perform day-to-day marketing activities, but may not have the expertise to perform a high-level marketing strategy. This is similar to a person who hires an attorney to resolve legal issues. A business organization hires a consultant to provide expert advice and counsel.

To perform a project. A multi-location regional hospital would like to develop a new software application that will allow them to track their accounts receivable from insurance companies. They contract with a consulting firm to meet with their internal subject matter experts to define the full set of requirements, develop the new system, implement it, provide training to their staff, and support any issues with the application for a specified period of time.

Augment staff temporarily. A national retail company is developing a point-of-sale application that requires twenty programmers over a ten-month period. They currently have ten programmers available on staff. Rather than permanently hire an additional ten programmers they will contract with a firm to bring in ten programmers to supplement their team for the duration of the project.

Chapter 1 - Getting In

E very consulting firm has its own process for recruitment so it does little good to provide a specific recipe for a how-to guide to get hired in your chosen firm. Consulting firms generally look for people with the following characteristics:

A consultant that can think on his or her feet. Consultants are put in situations that require fast thinking and must not get flustered with difficult questions or confrontational situations. A firm wants to know that if you are in this situation you will not back down. At the same time, they want to ensure you won't respond confrontationally and potentially damage a client relationship.

Strong communication skills. As odd as it sounds, many people I've interviewed--whether right out of college or with years of experience--have difficulty with basic English grammar. A consultant needs to have the ability to speak and write succinctly to provide information to a client efficiently. This skill, within itself, helps instill confidence from the client that you know what you're talking about.

Leadership skills. Firms may ask you about your past experiences when you were in a leadership role. They will look for situations when you took charge in a group setting and influenced a group of people to accomplish an objective. They will look for your ability to make decisions under pressure.

Self-confidence. Perhaps all of the above items imply a high level of self-confidence, but firms look for people who can speak and act confidently. Be careful not to come off as arrogant. They will recognize arrogance as a façade for a lack of confidence.

Subject matter knowledge. Although consulting firms usually provide initial training to new hires, they want their recruits to have some knowledge that can be applied beginning with their first assignment. They are looking for college recruits with majors in practical knowledge, such as accounting, computer science, healthcare, and engineering.

When recruiting experienced candidates, they are seeking education and experience that will allow them to make an immediate assignment on a client project.

Tip #1: Determine Why You Want to Be a Consultant

Before you waste a lot of your time and that of the recruiting consulting firms, determine why consulting appeals to you. Some possible reasons include:

- You enjoy problem solving and believe consulting would be an exciting opportunity to develop deep experience in your chosen industry.
- You look forward to working with businesses to develop creative solutions to their problems.
- You like working in a project environment where many people come together to accomplish a common goal.
- You consider yourself a good leader and consulting is a great environment to apply your leadership skills.
- The variety of going from project to project and client to client is attractive to you.
- You are drawn by the challenge of working in a fast-paced, high-powered environment that demands you to do your best to succeed.

This is a question you will most likely be asked in an interview. There is no single correct answer. Of course, you have to back your statements up with facts. Be prepared to tell interviewers about your experience in problem-solving situations and what you liked about it. If you like to be challenged, tell them about specific times where you took on additional responsibilities in order to challenge yourself. Telling them what they want to hear without facts to back it up will fall flat.

There may be some selfish or personal reasons that you would like to pursue consulting. Reasons such as acquiring experience at a premier consulting firm in order to start your own firm or to get exposure to high-profile clients to obtain a job offer will not induce firms to hire you. Firms are looking for people who intend to be with them for the long term. If you are looking at consulting as a stepping stone your heart may not be in it. You will have a much lower chance of success as a result.

Tip #2: Determine the Type of Firm You Want to Join

Consulting is a broad term that covers a multitude of professional services. It runs the gamut from large, high-profile management consulting firms providing strategy consulting to Fortune 500 companies to an individual providing a temporary service to a sole proprietor. There are consultants for virtually every industry--healthcare, banking, retail, manufacturing, etc. All have industry specialists and almost every industry has sub-industry specializations. For instance, in manufacturing, there are specialists in automobile, heavy equipment, food manufacturing, etc. There are also industry generalists who provide professional services to all industries in areas such as human resources, information technology, and marketing.

After making the decision to enter consulting, determine the type of firm you'd like to work for.

The Tiers of Consulting

The consulting industry is often defined in terms of tiers based on size and industry influence.

Top-tier consultants are considered the elite of the industry and usually specialize in management and strategy consulting for all major industries. They have practices in many other areas including information technology and human resources. Top-tier firms include Boston Consulting Group, McKinsey & Co., Accenture, Ernst & Young, and PricewaterhouseCoopers.

Mid-tier consultants generally offer many of the same consulting services of the top tier, but are smaller in scale, usually less than $1 billion in annual revenues. Mid-tier firms often focus on mid-sized companies, but significant exceptions exist. Firms in this category include BDO, McGladrey, and Grant Thornton.

Industry-specific firms focus on a specific industry such as manufacturing or healthcare. There are thousands of firms of all sizes in this category.

Boutique consulting firms, also known as specialty consulting firms, have a focus in a particular area such as information technology, human resources, or marketing. This category also has many firms of various sizes.

Should you work for a large firm, put in two to three years to develop some wide-ranging experience and then move on to a firm that specializes in a specific industry? Or do you go right to the small boutique firm to develop a specialty in your first couple of years, then move on to a top-tier firm as a subject-matter expert in one particular industry or technology? The answer is that there is no standard formula for that career decision. Each type of firm--and each individual firm for that matter--has its pros and cons, which vary by individual. Something that you find interesting in a firm may sound like a prison sentence to someone else.

Each person needs to know enough about each option and decide which one provides the best fit for his or her interests and goals.

Tip #3: Prepare for Case Interviewing

Case Study:
In his last semester of his MBA program, Jeff was getting responses from recruiters for some top consulting firms.

He was having some lunch with his classmate Frank, who invited Jeff to join him and a few others that night to practice interviewing.

"Practice interviewing? Are you serious?" Jeff asked.

"Yeah, we get together about once a week and just bounce questions off of each other that the firms might ask."

"That's ridiculous," Jeff countered. "I've had a lot of job interviews before. I don't think I need any more practice." Jeff's next interview was the following Monday. He showed up a few minutes early in a well-pressed suit and a portfolio of résumés in case anyone needed an extra copy.

After a short wait in the reception area, a woman appeared through the mahogany door and called his name. She escorted him to a conference room down the hall. Three people were waiting for him at a round table. She introduced him to the waiting crowd. "This is Jeff Sullivan."

A middle-aged man spoke up first. He had a calm, easy-going voice. "Hi, Jeff. Have a seat. My name is Gary. This is Ann and Tony."

"Pleased to meet you," Jeff said as he shook each person's hand and accepted the seat across the table.

"This is the case portion of the interviewing process," Gary continued. "We'll be asking you about various business case scenarios. Just answer as clearly and as directly as you can. Here are some sheets of scratch paper if you need to use them."

In addition to his MBA, Jeff had eight years of experience at a major financial institution. He wasn't sure why he would need scratch paper. "Sounds good," He replied confidently.

Ann started out. "Jeff, let's say you have a client in the retail appliance business. Their current revenues are about two hundred million dollars a year. They lost about twenty million last year. They have about two hundred stores nationwide. What would you suggest they do to turn their business around?"

Stunned, Jeff quickly saw the need for the scratch paper. He grabbed the pencil and the top sheet of paper and asked, "Can you please give me those figures one more time?"

Ann repeated them as he wrote them down. But seeing the numbers was no help. He had no retail experience and had never even done a case study on one in any of his business classes. He sat there for a moment and finally said, "I'm not sure. I don't know much about retail. My background is in finance."

"Using your finance background, how would you approach it?" Gary asked.

Jeff stammered for a few minutes and finally said, "I'd look into some cost-cutting measures, perhaps close some stores that are bleeding the most money. Then I'd look for some options where I could invest in increasing sales."

"What types of options would you look into?" Ann shot back.

"I'm not sure. Maybe expanding inventory to provide more revenue options or investigate whether going to higher-end appliances could increase our margins."

The interviewing team realized that they wouldn't get much more out of Jeff on this one and Tony took a turn at asking. "Jeff, how many basketballs do you think would fit in this room?"

Jeff could only imagine how big his eyes got when he heard the question. "How many... basketballs did you say?"

"Yes, how many do you think it would take to fill this room?"

Why the hell do you care? Jeff wanted to ask. Instead he looked around and assessed the room. "I don't know, maybe a hundred or a hundred and fifty."

"How did you come up with that range?" Tony asked.

"It's just an estimate I guess. This seems like a room that could fit that many basket balls."

The interview went on for another hour. The team continued to ask Jeff questions about complex business scenarios with an occasional off-the-wall question like the basketball one. By the time it was over, Jeff was thoroughly flustered. At the close of the meeting, the interviewers thanked Jeff for his time and left the room.

Jeff left the firm's office building feeling fully deflated.

The next day, he saw Frank on campus. "How did the interview go yesterday?" Frank asked.

"Don't ask. I totally bombed it. Hey, you were talking about practicing for interviews last week. What do you do to practice?"

"We usually break out into pairs and ask each other case interview questions and practice answering them."

Jeff smiled, "You mean questions like 'How many basketballs would it take to fill this conference room?'"

Frank laughed, "That's a good one. Did they ask that one yesterday?"

"Yes, and a bunch of others I couldn't answer."

"We're meeting tomorrow night. Why don't you stop by? Wear a suit like you're coming to a real interview."

Jeff was a little surprised by that, but said, "Okay."

The next night, Jeff showed up at the library conference room. After introducing Jeff to the rest of the team, they split up into small groups and disbursed to practice mock interviews. Frank took Jeff with him just to observe for the night. Frank was paired off with Clair and they took turns interviewing each other.

Clair started out. "Your client is a hospital in a major metropolitan area. They have decided that their strategy is to focus on quality of health care. How do you advise them?"

Frank responded with several questions, some of which she answered and some she pushed back asking him to make some assumptions. They went back and forth for about fifteen minutes. Jeff recognized at one point that Frank was analyzing the situation using Michael Porter's Five Forces industry analysis.

Finally, Frank provided his answer, suggesting they change their strategy from focusing on quality of health care to convenience and availability to all areas of the metropolitan area.

As the night went on, Jeff was shocked. They were asking each other questions just like he had experienced in his interview, but Frank and Clair were much better at handling them.

When the practice session was over, Jeff offered to buy Frank a beer. When they found a table and placed their order Jeff turned to Frank. "How do you know how to answer those questions?"

"Well, I've been practicing for quite a while. I also have a couple of books specifically about case interviewing," said Frank.

"I had no idea of the kind of questions I'd face in a consulting interview," Jeff replied. "You really opened my eyes tonight."

"I'll loan you the books and send you a couple links to some helpful websites. They have sample questions and suggestions on how to approach them. Read through them and then meet us again next week for the practice."

The case interview is an approach that many consulting firms use to test their candidates on a number of aspects. They want to see if you can think under pressure so they'll ask you questions that you couldn't have possibly prepared for.

Additionally, they want to test your ability to think things through logically. They'll give you a question and try to see what kind of follow-up questions you ask to formulate the problem in your head. Then they will watch the logical process you go through to get your answer.

There may also be some basic calculations to see how well you can calculate things in your head. The primary objective for the firm is to determine if you can solve problems without getting flustered.

There are three main categories of questions. The most common is the basic business scenario question.

That's usually a question that presents a client and their business situation. They'll describe a challenge your fictional client is facing like new government regulations or an increase in fixed costs and ask you how you would advise them.

The second category of question they might ask is an estimating question such as, "How many basketballs would it take to fill this room?" With a question like this, they obviously aren't looking for the true answer. Again, they want to see your ability think when you're on the spot, come up with an estimate and develop an approach to solving the problem.

They will be paying attention to the assumptions that you make. If you state out loud the assumptions that a basketball is about twelve inches in diameter, that the room is about ten feet by ten feet, and that the room is about ten feet tall, then the answer is one thousand basketballs. But by not asking, you implied the assumption that the furniture has been removed and that the basketballs are inflated.

The third category of question is a logic question. Here they might ask a question like, "How many times in a day do the hands of an analog clock overlap?"

One might assume that they cross once every hour and just throw out "twenty-four" as the answer. But during the eleventh hour and twenty-third hour, they overlap at the end of the hour, which is part of the next hour. So the answer is really twenty-two. Here they also want to observe how you think about the details and consider all possibilities rather than how quickly you can come to an answer.

Candidates should prepare by studying books and websites and practicing with peers in real-world interview situations.

Tip #4: Focus on the Job, Not the Compensation

Case Study:

Chris was highly recruited out of college by many major management consulting firms. He had a 3.8 GPA and, as a member of the football team and president of his fraternity, he had a lot of team and leadership experience. As a result, he had his choice of firms with which to interview. The first two firms invited him to their offices for a full day of interviews, lunch with two vice presidents, and a dinner with the senior vice president of recruiting. They nearly fell over themselves praising him and did everything but present him with an offer. They touted their benefits, including their efforts to limit travel for their consultants. They emphasized that many of their consultants work from home when not assigned to a client project.

The third firm Chris interviewed with was his first choice. They were based in his home town and had the best reputation in his specialty area of study. This firm's recruiting approach was to make the recruit understand their business. Their philosophy was that the more a candidate understood about their culture and business approach, the better he would be able to determine whether he would like working at their firm. As a result, they concentrated on giving Chris a "day-in-the-life" overview in which he shadowed various people in the firm for different periods of time throughout the day.

At the end of the day, he met with a vice president for dinner. The purpose of this dinner was to assess Chris's impression of the firm. If he still had a favorable opinion, they would move on to the next step of more in-depth interviews. Chris was impressed with the firm and still held them at the top of his list. He was disappointed that they hadn't shared any information on their salary or benefits. At dinner, he began asking the vice president about the starting salary range for their recruits and whether there was much travel involved. He also wanted to know if they had work-from-home arrangements.

The vice president was equally disappointed in the aspects of the job that Chris focused on. He would have been much more impressed if Chris had focused on the consulting business, typical projects that they manage, and the culture within the firm. After conferring with the recruiting team the next day, they decided not to go to the next step in the interview process with Chris.

Three days later, Chris was shocked to receive a letter from the firm thanking him for his time and explaining that they had no positions that matched his qualifications.

Salary and benefits should not be discussed by the candidate during the interviewing process. Firms may tout some of their benefits as selling points, but it is best to maintain a game face. It is more impressive to the firm to show interest in the roles and responsibilities of the job and show that you are interested in their firm for the work rather than the compensation.

Once an offer is made, they have made a commitment to you. They will provide you with their salary offer and the full benefits package. This is the appropriate time to ask about specific benefits without risk of turning them away.

Tip #5: Sell Yourself

The résumé is a tool to get you in the door for an interview, but the firm is hiring you, not your résumé. When interviewing, it is important to sell yourself to the firm. A significant factor for success in consulting is the ability to sell a solution to a client. Supplement the information on your résumé to show them your full value.

When a firm proposes on a project with a prospective client, it is much like a job interview. They describe their capabilities in the hope that the prospective client will hire the firm. A job interview is like an audition for proposing on a project. If you can't sell yourself, they may assume you also won't be able to sell a project.

When telling the interviewer about your past experience, focus less on the tasks that you completed and more on the benefit it produced. State benefits in measureable terms, if possible. For example, if you waited on tables to help pay for college expenses, provide the percentage or total dollars of college funding that you were able to contribute. Or, if you volunteered for a fundraising effort, rather than telling them how many hours you worked, describe the benefit in terms of dollars raised or saved for the organization.

Proving to the firm that you have both the technical skills to do the job and the ability to sell will give them a compelling reason for wanting you on their team.

Tip #6: Do Your Homework

Case Study:

At the campus job fair Ryan impressed the top-tier consulting firm. He had a professional résumé that touted excellent grades and a lot of leadership experience.

He seemed confident and comfortable in the screening interviews and they were anxious for him to visit their offices for a day of interviews. He shared their eagerness.

On the night before the interview, he flew to their headquarters in Chicago. When he checked into the hotel room, he opened his laptop to do a little research on the firm. He perused their annual report, not really finding anything interesting. He got bored and started flipping through the channels on TV.

The next day, he went into the interviews confidently. The first person he talked to was a senior manager who introduced herself as Samantha Sullivan. She worked in the firm's strategy practice. She asked him several questions about his leadership experience and how he would handle various real-world business scenarios.

He was proud of his answers and she seemed pleased as well. Her follow-up questions seemed to agree with his answer and delve for more information.

When she had exhausted all of her questions she thanked him and asked if he had any questions for her.

"You said you're from the strategy practice, right?"

"That's correct," she answered.

"What other practices do you have at the firm?" he asked.

She hesitated for a moment. Then she answered, "Well, we have a number of practices. In addition to strategy, we have an IT practice, finance, operations, and M&A. There are actually nine practices. You can check our website to get the full list and what they're all about."

"Do you have branches in any other cities?"

"Yes, we actually have nineteen branch offices across the U.S. Again, all the locations are on our website." She paused for a moment and said, "Ryan, can I give you some advice?"

"Sure."

"These questions are all information you could find out by looking at our website. That's probably something you should have done before the interview. The next company you interview with, I would suggest you study their website and do some basic research on the firm before you interview with them."

Ryan's face felt hot. He was not only embarrassed, but angry at himself. He knew he had just blown the interview. He went through the remaining two interviews like a trouper, but he knew he was just biding his time.

That night on the plane back to school he kept replaying Ms. Sullivan's advice over and over in his head. He knew better than to not research the company.

Before any interview, it's important to do thorough research on the company you will meet with. This includes, but is not limited to:

The company's website. Read all of the main pages of the website. Take note on their lines of business and read as many of their blog entries as possible. Download and listen to their podcasts and write down any follow-up questions you may have about them.

Annual Report. If the company is a publicly traded company, their annual report can be found online. Read it thoroughly to learn how they communicate with their investors.

Google search. Doing a simple Google search will give you information from external sources. Some sites provide a forum for current and former employees to describe what it's like to work there. You can find online articles and blogs that provide unbiased information that you can't find on their website.

Prepare. Once you've read as much information as possible about the company, take some time to absorb it. Take notes and come up with intelligent questions that will inform you more about the company that could not be learned online.

Interviewing with a consulting firm is competitive business. During an interview, the firm may evaluate you on any interaction to come to a decision between you and the many other candidates. Showing them that you've done your homework by asking intelligent questions may not convince them to hire you. But it may stop them from eliminating you from contention.

Tip #7: Business Travel Is not Pleasure Travel

Case Study:
In an interview with a recruiting firm, Lauren went in with confidence and felt she was answering the interviewer's questions with ease. The interviewer was in her third year of consulting and described her experiences to Lauren. She had spent about two months in San Francisco and then four more in Denver. She wanted to know if Lauren would be able to work at a place that required this much travel.

Lauren explained that this sounded exciting. She loved travel. She had just gone to Florida with her boyfriend this past winter and they enjoyed going to different places and trying new restaurants. She went on to discuss the sight-seeing they had done and how much she enjoys seeing new cities.

The interviewer explained to her that business travel was quite different. She said that although you occasionally get out to see parts of a new city, most of the time is spent working at the client. There is not a lot of time left for sight-seeing.

In most consulting organizations, you generally go where the client is so travel is the norm. In the age of cost cutting, telecommuting, and heightened airport security, firms have reduced travel, but it is still prevalent. When consultants do travel, they are usually expected to maximize as much value from it as possible. While out of town, they usually stay at a hotel close to the client and work until well into the evening. Lunch and dinner at their desk is common and little of the new city is seen other than the airport, the hotel, and the client site.

Showing an expectation of business travel being enjoyable and pleasant shows a naiveté of business travel that may prompt them to take a pass. A more appropriate response from Lauren might have been to explain that she is aware that there could be significant travel, and that it is not an issue. Then, asking the interviewer about the work she did at those clients would show that she is more focused on the work than the inconvenience of travel.

This needs to be an honest statement. If you are unable or unwilling to travel, then it would be best to identify a consulting firm that focuses only on a local client base.

Chapter 2 – Client Relations

In the professional services industry there is no tangible product that can be held by the customer. The firm may have proprietary processes and templates in an effort to brand their service offering, but their service providers--their consultants--are drawn from the same talent pool that their competitors draw from.

Sustainable strategic advantage is achieved by taking all of your resources and combining them in a unique way that adds value to your end-consumer. Firms do this by establishing their unique blend of service offerings, smart hiring, and employing creative, ambitious individuals with extensive knowledge in these service areas. Then they train them to deliver it in a consistent manner.

Despite all of this effort, the most successful firms obtain business--and maintain it--through the relationships they develop with their clients. When a firm proposes for a new project, the client prospect will judge them on their perceived capabilities based on their discussions and the firm's past experience. When competing firms have comparable abilities, the decision often comes down to the firm with which the client feels they have developed a better working relationship.

Once a firm wins their first project at a client, their goal is to make them an annuity client and perform additional projects for them. The best way to do that is to provide excellent service. In addition, the firm wants to continue to develop a relationship with the client. This comes about by teaching their consulting staff to fit in to the client's culture and treating the client and their employees with respect. It is always beneficial to take the time to get to know and understand the client and their staff.

Tip #8: Determine the Client's Definition of Success

Case Study:
As the project came to a close, Kevin was filled with self-satisfaction. Even after factoring in requirements changes and the additional scope that was added to his consulting project, he managed the project to complete on time and well under budget. Based on the parameters his firm had established, he was in line to get a nice project bonus.

His final status meeting would be primarily a post-mortem. The system had been in production for a week now and there had only been only a few glitches.

To kick the meeting off, Kevin summarized the deployment efforts and the issues they had run into since going into production. "Other than these few small issues, things are running smoothly," he concluded.

"Small issues?" Sue, the client manager, questioned back. "I don't think that missing files are a small issue."

Kevin kept his composure. "Yes, we missed loading three production files on Saturday's deployment, but we identified them on Monday morning and had them deployed in an emergency deployment by Monday afternoon."

"Because of that, our e-commerce website was down for several critical hours," Sue continued. "We lost a lot of sales revenue during that period and we may have permanently lost customers. I don't view that as a small issue. Kevin, you were so focused on getting the project deployed on time that, in your rush, you missed getting everything we needed into production. In order to stay on budget, you sent everyone home Saturday before doing the due diligence of verifying that everything got done in time. I'm very disappointed."

Kevin wasn't sure what to say. He hadn't realized the ramifications of the missing files and was shocked that Sue wasn't as pleased as he was with the conclusion of the project.

When starting any client engagement, a critical step is to have the client define their view of the project's success. Consultants tend to get caught up in the metrics that the firm sets for project success from their own financial perspective. The client may have a much different opinion.

Throughout the project, continue to monitor the client's definition of success for the engagement. If their focus changes, the consultant may need to work on resetting the client's expectations or on refocusing the objectives of the team in order to achieve project success.

Tip #9: Focus on the Client's Best Interest

Case Study:
Toby's project with her client was winding down. It had been a successful project and her client manager, Dale, wanted to discuss plans for future work. Toby saw that as a vote of confidence in her and her firm.

"One of the things I'd like to start investigating is a business intelligence application for our sales team," Dale started out.

"I think that's a good idea," Toby said. "Your sales staff is large enough to benefit from that now."

"What do you think it would take?" asked Dale.

"Our firm doesn't have any experience in BI, but I know a firm that has done a significant amount of work in it. I'll also ask around so you have a few to choose from."

"This could be a pretty large project, Toby. Wouldn't your firm like to get involved?"

Toby paused. "Don't get me wrong Dale. We want to do business with you. But there are things we're very good at and things we don't know much about. We don't feel it serves you well to charge you while we're learning on the job. We'd rather help you find a firm that can do it right."

"When we were talking about staffing for our current project," Dale said, "your firm suggested the need for five developers. But you didn't even flinch when we decided to use subcontractors from another placement firm."

"Like I said," Toby stated, "we're interested in getting the job done right for you. If we focus on that, we know that we'll have you as a long-term client.

Many firms do their best to increase the billings on every project, using tactics like loading the team unnecessarily with their own consultants or over-stating their experience to win projects they don't have the expertise to do. They end up charging the client for the time it takes their team to learn how to do the new work.

Firms sometimes get away with charging their clients like this in the short-term. Clients end up with fee fatigue after being bled dry for so long.

Firms that think long-term keep their client's best interests in mind. Maintaining focus on the client's success is the best way to insure a long-term relationship which results in long-term success for both the client and the firm.

Tip #10: You're a Consultant, Not the Client

Case Study:
René entered the conference room and sat down across from Jared. She knew this was going to be one of those difficult coaching sessions. After a little forced small talk, she got to the point of the meeting.

"Jared," she said, "the reason I asked you here is that we have a little bit of a client perception problem."

"In what way?" Jared asked.

"Quite frankly, I'm a little disappointed with some of your behavior lately," René said.

Jared seemed confused and a little shocked. René could tell he didn't realize there was an issue. "What's been wrong with my behavior?" he asked with a little defensiveness.

"I can give you a couple of examples," René said. First, last week I asked you to provide that marketing plan for the client's new product. You had committed to having it to us on Wednesday. But you didn't submit it until the end of day Thursday."

"There was a lot more to it than I thought. I worked past midnight to get it done." Jared was getting more defensive now.

"I understand that, but I would have expected you to communicate those issues if you were going to be late delivering it. The client has also commented about the fact that you have missed a few of the daily stand-up meetings because you got in late. And in some of the requirements meetings you've seemed a little... disconnected."

"I'm a little surprised that they're complaining about those things," said Jared. "Several people on the client team have missed more meetings than I have. And they're never on time with any of their deliverables. I've had to ask them multiple times for documents. They usually average being about a week late on most of the documents they get to us."

"I realize that," said René patiently. "But as consultants, we're held to a different standard."

"That doesn't seem fair," Jared protested.

"Look," René said. "Clients hire consultants for a lot of different reasons. Sometimes they're looking for an expert in some area, sometimes they just need more staff than they can hire. But in almost every case, they're looking for people who will go the extra mile to get something done; more so than their regular employees will go. If you want to be held to the same standard as their employees, you could become an employee. My bet is you'll take a pay cut to do that."

Jared nodded slowly.

"But if you want to be a consultant, you have to deliver on your commitments and be committed at all times. You just can't be so casual."

Jared's expression revealed that he didn't like being held to a different standard. But he realized that she was right. "I understand," he finally responded.

When working at a client site, consultants sometimes have the tendency to assume a "When in Rome, do as the Romans do" attitude. They don't realize that they're really not Romans.

A large part of developing strong client relations is the many small things a consultant does in his basic daily behavior. Even when the client employees show a casual or lackadaisical attitude, the consultant can't assume the same mind-set.

Customer service needs to remain a priority regardless how the client's employees approach their work.

Tip #11: Develop a Thick Skin

Case Study:
Grant smiled to himself as he hit "Send." The architectural design he had developed for the client was the product of a significant amount of work on his part. He was sure the client would appreciate the level of detail he had put into it.

Grant was a little surprised that a company of his client's size didn't have better designs in place. But he had seen this before. As companies grow, they don't always grow their technical infrastructure with it. Before they know it, they're working on out-of-date technology. Grant was sure that his design would bring them into the twenty-first century.

The next day, Kumar, the client's technical lead, asked Grant to meet with him. Anticipating praise, Grant walked in with his head a little higher than usual. He was a little surprised to see two other tech leads sitting there with Kumar's boss, Bob.

"You missed the mark on this architectural design," he said before Grant had completely sat down.

Grant was stunned. "How so?" he could only get out.

"More than half of it has already been documented internally. You went way too far into detail in sections three through five. We already had that."

"I wasn't aware of that," Grant said. "Where is that existing documentation?"

"It's in our repository," was all that Kumar would give him. "I'd like you to go back and rewrite it so that it's usable for our group. I'm not very happy that we're paying you over two hundred dollars an hour to rewrite what we already have."

Grant left in a daze. He had worked so hard on that document and he was humiliated in front of his peers.

When he had regained his composure, he went back to his desk and began searching the client's repository of technical documentation. Despite an hour of searching, he found no existing technical designs that even resembled a duplicate of what he had submitted.

He finished his search and decided to talk it over with Bryan, his project manager, over lunch.

Over a burger and fries, he explained the meeting he had endured with Kumar and the strange group of attendees. Bryan listened and a wry smile formed on his face.

"Don't worry about missing the mark on the design, Grant. You didn't miss the mark, you exposed Kumar politically," said Bryan.

"What do you mean?"

"I saw your design. It exposed what a poor design they already had. That makes him look bad in front of his peers and his boss."

"That wasn't my intention," said Grant. "I was just trying to give them a better design."

"I know that and you know that," said Bryan. "So does Kumar. He'll probably implement your design. He just needed those people to think that he was more involved in it than he really was."

"I don't care if he takes credit for the whole design. Why did he have to humiliate me in front of those guys?"

"It was either you or him that got humiliated. He just needed you to take the fall for it," said Bryan.

"Was there something I could have done differently?" asked Grant.

"The only thing I would suggest is not taking it so personally and getting so upset. Every once in a while we have to take the fall for something the client did or didn't do," Bryan replied.

Clients can be critical for any number of reasons. Because of the rates they are paying the consultant, they may have a very high standard for the quality of work that they expect.

Sometimes, they simply offer constructive criticism in an effort to improve the consultant. Depending on how it is delivered, the consultant may take it personally.

Every once in a while, a consultant becomes a scapegoat for something a client didn't do or did wrong. They may blame you to deflect blame from their superiors or they may just be overly critical of your work.

Part of being a consultant is being able to deal with criticism and moving on rather than dwelling on it. No one enjoys criticism or ridicule. But a good consultant is able to let it roll off her back.

Despite the management style of the client or manager you work for, it's important to develop a thick skin when it comes to criticism. You will receive it for the rest of your career. If you let criticism destroy you, it gladly will. Consider the criticism doled out to people like the president of the United States, professional athletes, and professional sports officials. Their criticism is very public and can be very harsh and personal.

Criticism you receive from a manager or client will most likely pale in comparison.

If negative comments from the client become habitual or abusive, management at the consulting firm should be made aware. When a consultant is faced with an abusive client, it is imperative for the firm to be supportive and intercede to stop an abusive situation.

Tip #12: Beware of Silent Saboteurs

Case Study

Holly sat in the conference room with two of her fellow consultants. It was ten minutes past the meeting's scheduled start time and Sam was a no-show once again.

"This is the third time he's blown us off," she said in exasperation. "I wonder what the deal is."

She adjourned the nonexistent meeting and walked over to Sam's office. He was at his desk talking to one of his developers. "Hey, I'm sorry," he said. "We had an emergency production issue come up. Can we reschedule?"

"I'll see if I can reschedule sometime," Holly said without commitment.

That afternoon Alex, the partner from her firm, stopped by at the client and she sat down with him to discuss Sam.

Alex's interest piqued when he heard about Sam's behavior. "In the meetings he does show up for, has he shown any form of disruptiveness?" he asked.

"Now that you mention it, he asks a lot of questions. He kind of shoots ideas down but in a subtle kind of way," she responded.

"That's interesting," said Alex. "He may be quietly sabotaging the project. Has he handed in any deliverables late?"

"I've only asked him to provide two deliverables. They were both late and one had to be completely redone. Do you think he's doing this on purpose to damage the project?"

"We can't make that accusation," said Alex. "He's very busy so everything we have on him could be explained by the fact that he's spread so thin. But, whether he's doing it on purpose or because he's so over-allocated, the fact remains that it's an issue because it's bringing the project down."

"But this project is supposed to increase the productivity for his area. Why would he be intentionally disruptive?" wondered Holly.

There are many situations where a client employee will wreak havoc on a project. Sometimes, that person is so busy they are unable to attend meetings and provide information on a timely basis.

Other times, they may be clandestinely working to derail the project. This can happen for several reasons:

Fear of job loss. Consultants generally help client organizations become more efficient. This often translates to staff layoffs. If a software system can be installed that allows the client to do the same work with fewer employees, why wouldn't they eliminate jobs once the software is implemented? The employees may create disruptions in the project to reduce the chance of layoffs.

Resistance to change. Even if the client employees don't fear losing their jobs, they may fear that the completion of the project will cause an unwelcome disruption in their daily routines. Perhaps they fear being moved to a different location working with different people. Fear of the unknown can drive people to resist, causing major disruptions in a project.

General disdain for consultants. Client employees often dislike consultants. Perhaps they see them as outsiders who don't know the business as well as a full-time employee does. Perhaps a consultant from a previous job caused the employee to lose his job. Maybe it's just fun for them to disprove the experts. For whatever the reason, they may adapt a passive-aggressive approach in which they act friendly and cooperative on the surface, but work behind the scenes to bring the project--and as a result, the consultants--down.

The arsonist and the fireman syndrome. Some employees simply like to be the hero. When a big project is being executed that has executive attention, some workers will cause small disruptions, which culminate in major delays. They respond by swooping in to save the project, resulting in kudos by the executives. No one realizes that they actually set the fires that they heroically fought.

Tip #13: Learn the Client's Problems Before Solving Them

Case Study:
Russell stood in front of the room full of people. He had been giving sales presentations for a long time, but he still got just a little nervous before each one. That's okay, he thought. It keeps me on my toes.

"Good morning," he started out. "Thank you for your time this morning. I'm here to tell you how Truman Consulting Group can be your problem solvers of choice."

Russell went on to tell the group of prospective clients how much experience his firm had working with companies in their industry. One of the PowerPoint slides he showed them listed at least three of their direct competitors. "Truman Consulting has been working in this industry for a long time," he said.

He went on to explain how his firm had worked with one of their competitors to increase sales revenue by fifteen percent. Their assistance in implementing a sales force optimization system made a significant effect on sales for their previous client.

Russell's presentation lasted forty minutes. When he finished, he opened the floor to questions. There were a couple of generic questions from the group, but none that showed a deep interest in his presentation.

The majority of the meeting attendees filed out, politely thanking Russell and his team for his presentation.

Anthony Stevens, Russell's contact with the prospective client, stayed back, closing the door after his last peer left the conference room. He turned and sat down at the conference table across from Russell and his two colleagues.

"Well, how did you think it went?" Russell asked.

Anthony looked at him and paused. "Actually, I think you missed the mark."

Russell frowned. "What makes you think that?"

"We have an SFO system. It's working fine and our sales numbers are at an all-time high. Our problem is in operations. Because our sales have grown so much, we need to reengineer for better operational efficiency."

"We have a lot of experience in operational improvements, too," replied Russell. "I wish I had known that."

"I thought you might have asked us about it in this meeting," Anthony said. "Unfortunately, I don't think you won over any of the decision makers today."

Consulting is generally about solving problems for the client. It's important to know the right problem to solve. Consultants are often eager to demonstrate their experience and ability, but fail to determine the client's real problem.

A better approach is to make the initial meeting about the client rather than the consultant. Instead of touting your own experience, ask the prospective client to discuss their biggest challenges.

Once a consultant understands the client's issues, they can begin formulating solutions that are more customized to the client. The client wins by having their specific issues resolved.

The consultant wins by developing a loyal client that sees him as a trusted advisor.

Tip #14: Consider Yourself an Outsider

Case Study

On her first day at the client site, Heather saw the posters on the hallway bulletin boards publicizing the company's annual employee cookout. It was to be held the following Friday in the company parking lot. There was going to be lots of good food, door prizes, and employee recognition awards. She thought it would be a great opportunity for her to get to know her teammates in a more informal client setting.

When Friday rolled around she went down to the parking lot with the client employees and got in line for food. She sat with the employees that she had been working with over the previous week. They seemed polite, but a little uneasy with her presence. Each person who went through the line had been given a raffle ticket with a number. As they ate, the president of the company announced the numbers for door prizes. Finally, he called out the number that matched Heather's ticket. She went up to the stage area and found that she won a tablet computer. She was thrilled to actually win something and thought it was a generous prize. When she returned to her table, she was disappointed that her client teammates didn't share her happiness. She thought they were actually a little jealous.

On Monday morning, her account manager stopped by and asked to talk to her in the conference room. She explained to Heather that the client had raised an issue about her attendance at the company cookout on Friday. The purpose of the cookout was a morale boosting activity to thank employees for their dedication to the company. They didn't mean to be exclusionary of consultants, but it was intended for employees only. She explained that it put everyone involved in an awkward situation.

Heather was both embarrassed and ashamed. She hadn't thought about the purpose of the event and felt bad that she took a prize that should have gone to an employee. She apologized to the account manager, but the damage had been done. They both agreed that apologizing to anyone at the client would create more awkwardness. They marked it as a lesson learned and decided to move on.

In addition to the standard benefit offerings of health insurance, retirement savings programs, and vacation time, most companies provide informal employee benefits. These include events such as company picnics, golf outings, and discounts on their products.

Consultants are sometimes included in these employee activities, but it cannot be assumed. In many cases, consultants are considered outsiders and held to a different standard. You are not an employee of the client and it can't be assumed that you share in the informal employee benefits. It depends on the client whether it is acceptable for an external consultant to participate. Before participating in any informal client-sponsored activities, make sure you are invited. Moreover, if they invite you, it is usually proper etiquette to attend.

Client employees are also often allowed privileges such as selling candy bars as fund raisers for their child's sports team, bringing their children to work with them if they have a daycare issue, and dressing for Halloween. These scenarios are rarely appropriate for a consultant to do at a client site. The client pays a high hourly rate for a consultant's time and expects him to be focused on his work without such distractions.

Bottom line: Make sure you know your place and error on the side of caution.

Tip #15: Don't Make the Firm Look Bad

Case Study:

Diane, a senior manager with her consulting firm, had been on a client site for a project to analyze the client's current vendor relationships. They needed to determine whether they could reduce the number of vendors for more efficiency. Her firm sold the client on their analysis methodology, which was more expensive than their competitors', and included a formal scoring process for each vendor based on several objective factors including their long-term viability, knowledge of the client's industry, and their delivery capabilities. Diane also met with each vendor's account managers and members of their implementation teams. In the process, she developed personal opinions based on her like and dislike of each firm's representatives.

Robb, the client executive, wanted to reduce the number of their vendors and wanted to know the findings indicating which vendors could be eliminated and with which ones to consolidate their business. In a meeting with the client's senior management to discuss her findings, Robb asked her, "Based on your analysis, which software vendors can we consolidate functionality and which ones can we begin phasing out?"

"Would you like to know my opinion or the firm's opinion on that?" she asked in response. She then explained that, although the tool they use to assess each firm's ability to support the client's needs provided them with one set of results, she had her own opinions such as the vendor responsiveness and their general attitude. Much of this was based largely on her personal opinions of the individuals with whom she met.

Robb left the meeting confused. He wondered why he paid such a premium for their methodology if she was just going to undermine it with a different set of subjective information.

One of the main functions of a consultant is to facilitate decision making for the client. In order to do that, the information you provide to the client must be as objective as possible. Many firms have tools to assist in providing objective data to clients without being tainted with irrelevant data.

A consultant should be careful not to undermine a firm's tools or methodology with opinions or suggestions that contradict the results. This will hurt the firm's credibility with the client and, eventually, their own.

Care should also be taken to avoid undercutting opinions of fellow consultants. When providing formal client recommendations, team members should meet to discuss the data and form an agreed-upon solution. Not all members of the team will agree at all times. In these situations, the most senior member of the team will decide the approach. At that point all team members, whether they agree with the decision or not, need to support the decision so that the firm is consistent in their communication. If a client points out an inconsistency between your opinion and that of a fellow consultant, back out of the conversation gracefully until you can confer with the other consultant before discussing the issue with the client any further.

Tip #16: You May Be Viewed as the Enemy

Case Study:

Carla was excited about her new project assignment. She was a project manager implementing an Electronic Medical Records (EMR) application at a major hospital. She planned the kick-off meeting with several key physicians, nurse practitioners, and administrative staff. Most of them arrived late and their body language indicated that they weren't happy to be there.

As she started the meeting by giving an overview of the system and the timeline of the project, there were several complaints that the schedule was too aggressive. Throughout the meeting there were negative comments questioning the need for an EMR at their hospital. They also second guessed her firm's approach and didn't hold back on their condescending heavy sighs over many of the details of the application.

It didn't get any better once the project went into full swing. Few of the staff members were cooperative and some were blatantly disruptive. Although nobody on the staff did anything to openly sabotage the project, no one made any effort to ensure the project's success.

Carla tried her best to befriend people on the project, but got no response back. One day she had a one-on-one meeting with an administrative assistant. While they discussed the system's data entry interface and how much easier the Physician Order Entry module would be, the assistant asked, "How many of us do you think this system will replace?"

"I haven't heard any discussions about staff reductions," Carla replied. She went on to explain the reasons the hospital was implementing the EMR system, including providing higher quality healthcare and improving their efficiencies. The assistant explained to her that there were rumors that ten percent of the administrative staff would be fired and that physicians and nurses would be given more work as a result. It dawned on Carla that that was why there was so much resistance to the project from the staff.

Consultants are generally brought in by the client's senior management to assist them in solving a business problem. Often times, the solutions provided by a consulting firm result in unpopular changes. These changes can range from new organizational structures that disrupt employees' daily routines to efficiencies that result in the need for fewer employees, resulting in lay-offs. To a client's employees, consultants are often synonymous with bad news.

Too often, from the employee perspective, consultants are outsiders that come onto their turf and hold secret meetings behind closed doors with the executives. They huddle in their war rooms and strategize how to disrupt their jobs by cutting minutes off of processes and eliminate as many employees as possible to justify their inflated rates. They suspect IT consultants of conjuring up computer applications that automate processes to eliminate manual processing, again resulting in head-count reduction.

Even when consultants are brought in simply to augment the staff temporarily for a large project, employees often assume the consultant is there doing the same work as them, for more money. Consultants should be aware of these client concerns and focus on the benefits of the system to them. Above all, do not lie to them. If you know that there will be staff reductions, do not tell them that it won't happen. It's better to suggest they talk to their managers and focus on the project tasks.

Tip #17: Don't Make Yourself Too at Home

Case Study:

Marge was an employee at Harrison Securities, Inc. She sat in a cubicle adjacent to a conference room on her floor. Magnusson Consulting Group had been brought in to do a performance study and was given the conference room as a "war room" for the five consultants to do their work. After about a week, the consultants began getting to know each other better, becoming a cohesive team. They also began working late nights and ordering dinner in. As a result, they got more comfortable with each other, joking around, discussing what they did over the weekend, and sharing personal stories with each other. As the comfort level increased, so did their volume.

Marge began noticing that she could overhear their conversations, but it didn't bother her at first. As the consulting team began to chat more often and with higher volume, it became a distraction. Marge often talked on the phone to customers and she wondered if they could hear some of the personal, sometimes inappropriate, conversations emanating from the nearby conference room.

Sometimes when she came to the office in the morning, she would see that they left remnants of their previous evening's dinner--pizza boxes, Chinese take-out containers, etc.--outside the conference room door intended for the cleaning people, who had evidently left for the night before the consultants. The odor of the stale-smelling food lingered for most of the day.

The final straw came when Cody and Michelle, two of the consultants, walked into the conference room from a confrontational meeting complaining about the incompetence and stupidity of Marge's boss, Jerry.

"That SOB Jerry has to be the biggest dumb ass I've ever met in my professional career," vented Michelle.

Marge estimated that Michelle was no older than twenty-five and wondered how many dumb asses she could possibly have met to date. And although she had her own personal questions concerning Jerry's gray matter, she thought it was inappropriate to say such things and unprofessional to say them so they could be overheard by client employees. She reported their behavior to her boss who wasted no time calling the firm's account manager.

When clients bring in a consulting team, they don't always have ample space for them to work. Consultants are often put in a conference room--usually the size of a large closet--as a "war room." Consultants frequently sit two or three to a cubicle designed for one person, or even sit at tables lined up along a corridor. Add to this that they are often treated as outsiders by the client's employees. A "we vs. them" mentality develops and causes them to develop a camaraderie that fosters a more casual environment among them.

Consultants are invited to client sites to perform work. It's always best to act as if you are a guest in the client's home by remembering the following things:

- Keep voices as low as possible. It avoids disturbing the client and keeps them from hearing things they don't need to hear.
- If a contentious conversation must be held, make sure it is not overheard. Close the door or move to another location out of earshot of others.

- Personal conversations should be held to a minimum and out of range, preferably in an off-site environment such as lunch.
- If any food is brought to the workplace, be mindful of the odor it can leave and dispose of all leftover trash in a place that will not bother others, such as in a cafeteria, break room, or outdoor dumpster.
- Avoid use of foul language or subjects that could be considered offensive to anyone overhearing. Contrary to what you may think, few people are all that interested in your sexual exploits or your political views.
- Never criticize the client's business operations, their facilities, or an employee of the client. Even if a client eavesdropper happens to agree, they may not appreciate an outsider's criticism.

Tip #18: Limit Personal Online Usage

Case Study:

Jim was a hard worker and worked long hours. He was on a project with a tight deadline and they were running behind. He had put in several thirteen-hour days and was also working on the weekends. He was well organized and, as a result, was a good multi-tasker. He always had several applications open on his computer at any given time and could switch from one to the other in a flash.

He also kept several tabs open on his web browser for sites that he used for both work and personal purposes. He would check his personal e-mails and Facebook three to four times a day. It never took more than a few minutes each time and, based on the hours he worked, he more than made up for it.

Dominic, a manager for the client, received an Internet usage report weekly from IT. Scanning the report for exceptions, he noticed that Jim's usage showed a large number of hits to Yahoo, Facebook, and several other sites that raised his eyebrow.

That afternoon when he met with Jim's account manager, Dominic showed him Jim's Internet usage report and asked why he was spending so much time on the Internet for personal usage. "Is this why you guys are behind on the project?"

After the meeting, the account manager took Jim to a conference room and chewed him a new one.

"What the hell are you doing on the Internet all day while we're all trying to get a project completed?"

Jim stared at him in disbelief. "I check personal stuff a couple of times a day. Why are they getting all bent out of shape over that?"

It's the rule more than the exception today that companies track Internet usage closely, particularly for consultants. Software is used to block inappropriate content such as pornography and dating and job search sites; however, other sites that may need to be used for legitimate business purposes are not blocked. These sites are allowed, but tracked for frequency, length of time visited, and context.

The best rule to follow is to only use the client's Internet access for legitimate business purposes. There are times when a commercial site needs to be accessed, for instance to order dinner when the team works late. A manager with the consulting firm or the client should be made aware so there are no surprises on the client's usage reports.

Clients may state that they block illicit sites, but don't track usage. That sets the expectation that if it isn't blocked, it's okay to access. That is not a license to surf the web. Regardless of the filters set up by the client or the sites the client's employees visit, use the client's Internet access sparingly and for business purposes only. If you have to use it to order a pizza or look up a phone number, keep a log of the times and purpose in case you're questioned about it.

Tip #19: Avoid Personal Activities

Case Study:
Cheryl had been on-site with her client for over a month. In that time, she had developed close relationships with several of the client employees. She had gone to lunch with the client manager she reported to and even went shopping with her a couple of times. As she got acclimated with the client's culture she saw that it was acceptable for employees to do personal activities such as hold personal conversations on their mobile phones and pay their bills at their desk. Before long, she felt comfortable doing some of the same things at her desk.

That Friday, when Izzy, her account manager, showed up for a status meeting, she pulled her aside and explained that they had reported overhearing personal conversations and seeing her doing personal activities at her desk.

Cheryl was stunned. "Their people do it all the time. Why are they singling me out for that?"

"It may be that they haven't seen their employees do it," Izzy replied. "But either way, clients usually give their employees more latitude than they give consultants. They're paying a lot more for you and the project that you are working on is much more critical to the company than what most of their employees are working on."

Cheryl understood Izzy's points, but she wasn't completely convinced. "The double standard just doesn't seem fair."

"Look at it this way. If you were hired to work for the client you may have a lot more freedom to do some of those things, but your salary would likely be lower and you might not get assigned to high profile projects like this. It's a tradeoff. Only you can decide whether it's worth it or not."

Client perception is a critical factor in consulting. From the client perspective, they are paying top dollar to have experts come in to perform a task. There is often a double standard between the way clients treat employees and the way they treat consultants. Clients have made a long-term commitment to their employees and may allow them some freedom to do personal activities on company time. They usually have a higher interest in their employees' morale and general happiness.

Consultants, on the other hand, are hired on a short-term basis, at a higher cost, to accomplish a specific objective. It is often a high-profile project that has executive attention. The client expects a laser-beam focus on that objective. Consultants should not do anything to give the impression that they are distracted, too casual, or in any way focused on anything other than the client's work.

Tip #20: Don't Use Client Resources for Personal Use

Case Study:

Takumi was an offshore consultant brought onshore for a two-month period to gather requirements and act as the subject matter expert (SME) for the offshore team. He was working at his desk one December afternoon and saw something he had never seen before. He looked out his window and saw snow for the first time in his life. He went outside and admired it, touched it, and picked some up to watch it melt in his hand. Then he took a few quick pictures with his phone. When he returned to his desk, he connected his phone to his PC, uploaded the pictures to his personal website, and e-mailed his friends back home to check the new pictures out.

The next morning, Takumi's account manager received a call from the client's security director. His network monitoring software had identified an upload of three images to an external IP address that was not on their approved list. He informed the account manager that the firm would be fined $5,000 for violating the security regulations that they signed as part of their Master Services Agreement.

That afternoon Takumi went back home with only some pictures of snow. He was fired the next day.

As stated before, you should act as though you are a guest while at a client site. This is just as important while using their computer equipment as their office space. Many companies monitor network usage closely and some have contractual requirements with their consulting vendors regarding what is, and is not, allowed. Management at the firm should review these regulations with the team at the beginning of a project and revisit them regularly so that no one is surprised. That will greatly reduce the chance of the regulation being violated and harming the client relationship.

Additionally, when joining a project, ask if the regulations have been documented. In any event, it's best to err on the safe side by using the client's equipment only for legitimate, project-related activities.

Tip #21: Client Employees Have Their Own Jobs to Do

Case Study:

Emily was consulting on a project at a major retail company in the role of business analyst. She was responsible for meeting with a cross-functional team of client employees to define requirements for their new application. She planned three two-hour meetings each week over a six-week period to which all twelve client team members were invited. In each meeting, she focused on a specific area of the business. Some of these focused areas had little or nothing to do with the business functions of some of the meeting invitees. Emily noticed that in some meetings, team members either left early or did not attend at all. She was concerned that they would miss important business rule definitions or that some definitions would be incomplete without the input of the full team.

In her weekly status report, she raised an issue that lack of full participation of the client's cross-functional team may adversely affect the quality of the application

The client manager replied that she had received feedback that the requirements gathering meetings were wasting a lot of their time because they discussed requirements that did not affect them. Many were, in effect, sitting through six hours of meetings a week with little opportunity to provide input or affect the design of the application.

When consultants are charged with executing a project at the client it is usually their single focus. Client employees usually get assigned to assist on the project, but it is rare for the project assignment to be full time. Instead, it is in addition to their other daily responsibilities. Consultants need to be respectful of their time and coordinate meetings and other responsibilities so that their time is utilized as efficiently as possible.

When working with a client team:

- Limit full-team meetings as much as possible. If the input of only a few team members is required, meet with only the necessary team members and provide meeting minutes to all team members to keep them up to date.

- When scheduling meetings with all team members, provide an agenda at least one day in advance, detailing which members of the team are critical to the discussion. This will allow each team member to decide if they need to attend. Again, meeting notes should be distributed to the full team.

- Be flexible with team members' ability to attend meetings. If they are unable to attend a meeting in which their input is critical, arrange a one-on-one session with them before the meeting to get their input so that it can be discussed in the meeting.

- Determine the commitment level of each team member at the beginning of the project. This should be an assumption detailed in the original consulting agreement. If any team member is unable to meet his commitment, the client manager should look into reducing his other commitments, or replacing him with someone that can carry out the responsibilities.

Tip #22: Keep Client Management in the Loop

Case Study:

Amanda was eager to get started on her new consulting assignment. She was the project manager on a marketing study at a major consumer products company. The client provided a team of eight employees to work with her four consultants to develop a marketing campaign. Steve Adams, the vice president of marketing, had hired Amanda's firm for this study and had hand-selected the team of employees to serve on the project.

As soon as Amanda received a client e-mail account, she scheduled a kick-off meeting with all of the team participants. She attached an agenda that included introductions, an explanation of the objective of the project, a proposed timeline, and responsibilities of each team member. The key team member that Amanda forgot was Steve. In addition to not being invited to the kick-off meeting, Steve had not yet met with each of his team members to ask them to participate or even to inform them of the upcoming project.

Steve got upset when he received an e-mail from one of the invitees asking about the meeting. He felt that Amanda had gone around him in scheduling the meeting without his approval. Steve also thought he should have been allowed input on the meeting's agenda.

Steve called Amanda and asked why she scheduled the meeting without his approval. He also wanted to know why he wasn't invited or allowed to review the agenda prior to it being sent out to the team.

Amanda was perplexed. She assumed when Steve gave her the list of names, that they had already been informed of the project and given their commitment. As an executive, she didn't think Steve would be interested in that level of minutia in the project. She asked why Steve would give her names of team members without having first obtained their commitment and directly questioned why he would be involved in such detail.

That was not a good move. Steve was even more angered now. He explained to her that he is responsible for the success of this project and it is imperative he be included in all of its activities.

Amanda tried to apologize, but it fell flat since she still felt she was right and that Steve was micro-managing. Amanda considered the project her rightful responsibility.

Every manager has her own style and expectation for involvement. Amanda made two big mistakes in this situation. First, she made assumptions on Steve's management style and incorrectly took for granted that he would not want to be involved in the kick-off meeting. In their first meeting, she should have asked Steve what level of involvement he expected on meetings and any team communication.

She should also have run her planned next steps by Steve to obtain his approval. Without knowing Steve's management style or his expectations, she should have sent a draft of the agenda to Steve for his input and suggest a kick-off meeting as a next step. This would have given Steve the chance to provide his own input to the agenda and hold off Amanda from scheduling a meeting until all planned participants had been informed.

Amanda's second mistake was not accepting responsibility for excluding Steve from the process. Regardless of Amanda's opinion of how involved Steve should be, as the client sponsor, it was Steve's decision. When Amanda received the call from Steve and learned that he was upset, her one and only response should have been to apologize, beg forgiveness, and ask for Steve's direction in correcting the mistake in a way that saved face for Steve.

Tip #23: Don't Flaunt Client Expenses

Case Study:

Mandy was on an out-of-town project for a healthcare firm. She flew from Chicago to their headquarters in San Francisco every Monday morning, returned home on Thursday evenings, and spent Fridays working from her home office. She reported all travel-related expenses on her weekly expense report. Her client reimbursed those expenses. Her five-person team went to dinner together once or twice a week and enjoyed trying different local restaurants.

They would often ask the client employees for suggestions for local restaurants. They would share stories of their dinners and restaurant critiques with client employees and managers the next day.

The employees knew that their company was paying, not only for the consulting team's hourly rates, but also for them to dine at some of the nicer restaurants in the area that they could not afford. After a while, they began to resent hearing about the dinners Mandy and her team enjoyed while the clients rushed home to cook dinner for their families.

Business travel is often glorified by people who don't travel. Somehow they get the impression that it's a vacation every week. The fact is that business travel is not very glamorous at all. Consultants are away from their families, friends, and significant others every week. They miss baby's first steps, ball games, and birthdays. They spend their weekends catching up on laundry and running errands they couldn't do while they were out of town.

Traveling on a weekly basis gets old quickly. Delays at airports, long lines, cancelled reservations, and lost luggage make for a great deal of wasted time and frustration. Added to that, living in a small hotel room alone three to four nights a week makes for a less-than-desirable lifestyle.

Perhaps the one perk to traveling is trying new restaurants on the client's dime. This actually happens less often than clients realize. When traveling to client sites, consultants usually log late hours to get a project done. The standard fare is take-out food eaten in a conference room.

When consultants do get a chance to dine out it is best to keep it to themselves. Clients have enough reasons to resent consultants. Flaunting dining at up-scale restaurants adds fuel to that fire. Additionally, client managers that approve consulting invoices don't need to be reminded that in addition to hourly rates, they're also paying for fancy dinners.

Tip #24: Lose the Battle, Win the War

Case Study:

Traci had a competitive spirit all of her life and always loved a challenge. She saw consulting as an excellent way to test her abilities. As a business analyst, she was assigned to a client to facilitate requirements gathering sessions and document business requirements for a new application. She took copious notes and had a sponge for a memory. The client liked this because she could identify inconsistencies in requirements definitions on the spot, which eliminated the need to do rework later in the project.

After all of the sessions had been held Traci documented the requirements. She obtained signoff from all the users for the application so the developers could begin their programming.

During the development and testing phases, questions often arose regarding the documented requirements. Traci easily answered them based on her notes and excellent memory of the conversations. When it came time for the user community to perform their User Acceptance Testing (UAT), they came upon a problem where the programs did not function as the requirements stated.

Traci was called into the meeting and they described the situation to her. The issue came down to interpretation. The business requirement in question was worded in a way that could be interpreted in two different ways. Traci--and the programmers--interpreted it in one way, while the users saw it in a completely different light. Having remembered the conversations about this requirement, Traci held her ground and refused to admit that she interpreted it wrong. This caused some bad feelings with the users and eroded a lot of the goodwill that Traci and her firm had built up over the past several months.

The issue was left at a stalemate at the end of the meeting. When Traci took it to her project manager, he decided that they should modify the programs to work the way the users saw it at no extra charge to the client. Traci was furious that he did not support her in his decision. She was certain that she had worded the requirement and interpreted it exactly as the users had specified in the requirements sessions.

Whether Traci was correct in regard to the requirement is irrelevant. As soon as Traci recognized that the issue was not with how the requirement was worded, but how the two parties interpreted it, the issue should have been tabled until she could discuss it with her project manager. It's often better to fall on your sword and do whatever it takes to resolve a problem at the firm's cost rather than risk hurting the client relationship.

The project manager has better visibility of the project finances and can take into account, among other things:

- How much contingency or extra built-in time is available for such situations.
- The amount of time required to make the correction.
- Whether they will harm the relationship with the client more by fighting back vs. making the fix.
- Whether they are setting a precedent for fixing anything the users happen to change their minds about.

Proving yourself right may give a temporary feeling of triumph, but it is always better to step back and look at the bigger picture to determine what the long-term effects are. Being stubborn seldom helps you win an argument or strengthen a client relationship.

Tip #25: Know the Client's Gift Policies

Case Study:

Joel was the project manager on a project for a new client and was eager to make a good first impression. He had scheduled a kick-off meeting with all of the client's project team members, including the executive sponsor team and several managers. Knowing that people like free stuff he arranged to get various items with the firm's logo for giveaways at the meeting. At every seat he placed a mouse pad, a coffee mug, and a mechanical pencil, each with the firm's logo emblazoned upon them.

As the team rolled into the meeting, most team members expressed joy at the gifts placed at the tables. The last person to come in was Margaret. Joel began asking the room to quiet down so he could begin going through the agenda. Margaret was a client manager that Joel had already found to be difficult during the initial planning stages.

She raised her hand and asked, "Are these items supposed to be for our employees?"

"Yes," Joel replied. "These are just some gifts from our firm for your folks."

"Perhaps you didn't know Joel, but we have a strict policy against accepting gifts of any value from our vendors. It is documented in our Loss Prevention Policy."

Joel was a little taken aback. He couldn't believe she would make an issue of such inconsequential items. He quickly apologized and explained that he was unaware of that policy. He told them they could leave the items on the tables and he would collect them and take them back to his office after the meeting.

The remainder of the meeting went without incident, but Joel felt deflated by being shot down in such an embarrassing manner. At the end of the meeting, after everyone left, he did the funeral march around the room, collecting his rejected offerings.

Most companies have policies regarding vendor gifts that are set at a dollar value threshold. Any gifts above a certain value must be either returned or reported to management. These policies are clearly to avoid conflicts of interest by bribing managers with valuable gifts or vacations in return for business contracts, but some clients have a no-tolerance policy for any gift giving. Determining the client's policies prior to the meeting and having the gift approved by management ahead of time would have saved Joel his public embarrassment.

Tip #26: Protect the Client's Confidentiality

Case Study:

Andy was a marketing consultant working at Polk Manufacturing. He had been on their account for well over a year and was helping to develop marketing plans for their new products. Polk had a new product for which they had recently applied for a patent. It was part of an exciting new line they hoped to introduce next year to leapfrog the competition.

It was difficult for Andy to hold in his excitement of the new product. If it did explode in the marketplace, like they all expected, this would be the beginning of a huge marketing contract for Andy and his firm. They would have the potential to beat out some of the other marketing firms that Polk currently used.

One Saturday evening, on the way to the movies, Andy told his wife Elaine about the Polk product and how excited he was about it. This could really be the boost to his career that he had been waiting for.

The next week, Elaine was at lunch with one of her friends at a local restaurant. As the conversation evolved to their husbands' jobs, Elaine told her friend about Andy's enthusiasm over this new product at Polk Manufacturing and how it could really catapult his career with the firm. At the next table sat Fred Garvin, the vice president of New Product Marketing at Polk Manufacturing, overhearing the entire conversation.

That afternoon, Fred went back to the office and summoned Andy. He explained what he had heard and fired Andy's firm on grounds that they violated their confidentiality agreement. Security escorted Andy and his team to the lobby.

Consultants are often privy to more confidential client information than many of the client's own employees. They are often contracted to work on high-profile projects and are required to sign confidentiality agreements. It is not always made clear what pieces of client information are confidential. Best practice is to assume all client information is secret unless you see it in their commercials or on their website.

The speed of word of mouth and the inability to control who may overhear information makes it difficult for you to monitor it. Always assume that *confidential* means it should not be discussed with anyone who does not have a reason to know. This includes spouses, children, friends, or even peers within your firm.

Confidential client information can be any of the following:

- Financial data
- Pending mergers or patents
- Unreleased marketing or strategic plans
- New store locations
- Layoffs
- Reorganizations

There may also be individuals within the client's company that are on a need-to-know status. Avoid discussing confidential information at the client site if there is a risk of being overheard. After meetings, pick up all papers left on the conference table.

Tip #27: Balance Consulting Standards with Client Standards

Case Study:

The requirements review session did not go well for Robin. While meeting with client team members, Tim and Joan, the subject matter experts for the client, focused more on the format of his document than the content. Robin was a stickler for detail, which made him an excellent business analyst in most cases. His firm's methodology provided a standard template for business requirements with sections for several scenarios and categories of information. He followed his firm's template to the letter.

Unfortunately, Tim and Joan were accustomed to their own format for business requirements. They had asked Robin to follow their format and had returned the document once before when their request had not been heeded. He made a few changes, but stuck primarily to the original format.

"This is very disappointing Robin," Joan said. "We specifically asked you to modify the requirements to meet our needs."

"This is our firm's standard," he explained to them. "If you review the document you'll find that it has all the information you need."

His format explained redundant details for each scenario of their process which caused them to read through duplicate information for many conditions. If there was a change to one scenario, they had to make sure that the change was made for each one. They tried to explain this and the resulting consequence that it cost them unnecessary time. He was adamant that this was the firm standard that they had paid for and he was unable to do it another way.

Most large consulting firms have their own methodologies, standards, and templates in an effort to provide their clients a complete and consistent approach to their service. Flexibility needs to be allowed to give the clients what they want. There is no such thing as a one-size-fits-all approach to consulting. Steps within a methodology may be inserted, removed, or modified in some way that provides client satisfaction. Documentation templates may need to be modified to comply with client standards or expectations.

Consultants are engaged for their expertise. Their standards and methodologies help them provide a consistent and branded service. Sometimes, it allows them to work more efficiently. These tools should not get in the way of providing expertise to the client in the formats that they desire.

Tip #28: Comply with the Client's Work Schedule

Case Study:

Progressive Consulting Services was performing a twelve-week strategy study at Lincoln Office Supplies. Although Lincoln followed a standard workday of 8:30 AM to 4:30 PM, the Progressive consultants usually didn't arrive until 9:00 AM. They almost always put in long days, staying well past 4:30 PM.

The Lincoln employees noticed the consultants' late arrival, but didn't say much at first. As the project progressed, the consultants were working longer days, sometimes until 10:00 PM. When this happened, they sometimes didn't come in the next day until 10:00 AM. Even though they were working ten- and twelve-hour days, Lincoln's employees only saw them strolling in to work an hour and a half after their workday began

It didn't take long for the Lincoln employees to show their frustration and resentment. They would stop by the war room at 9:30 AM to ask one of the consultants a question, only to find the room dark. They couldn't schedule a meeting before 10:00 AM for fear that the consulting team wouldn't be in yet. One employee made a comment to the project manager about them coming in so late. He responded that they worked so late he let them sleep in a little. The client employee wondered whether they would have to work so late if they just came to work on time.

Most clients have a set of written or unwritten rules within their culture that their staff follows. One of them is when the workday starts. Some begin early, at 7:00 or 7:30 AM, while others don't officially start until 8:30 or

9:00 AM. Seeing consultants roll in after the client employees have been there for over two hours doesn't sit well in their efforts for acceptance. The client does not see how late you worked the previous evening. The client wants face time with their consultants. To maximize it:

- Learn the client's standard work hours and be there during those hours.
- Even when working late into the evening, consultants must be available for meetings or questions during the client's normal business hours.
- When running late, make sure to call a manager to let him know, and don't allow it to happen on a regular basis.
- If the client is flexible enough, establish core work hours that allow for later arrivals and early leavers. For instance, core hours of 9:00 AM to 3:00 PM lets everyone know the window of time everyone should be available for meetings and questions.
- Schedule meetings during their work schedule. Scheduling meetings late in the day or after they normally leave, even though you plan to be there, will generate resentment.

Tip #29: Keep Cool Even When the Client Doesn't

Case Study:

The package selection project at a small manufacturing firm was on schedule. Two vendors had been invited to give product demos of their functionality to a selected group of users at the company. Lynn was the project manager for the consulting firm and Grace had assisted her in gathering requirements and using them to help pare down the list of vendors to the two that came for visits. After the half-day demo by the first vendor was complete, they felt it had gone well and went to meet with Wendy, the company's chief financial officer and sponsor of the project.

As soon as they walked into her office, they could tell she was upset.

"Is there a problem, Wendy?" Lynn asked.

"Oh, you bet there's a problem," she replied excitedly. "I just got done talking to three of our directors that attended that demo and they're mad as hell. None of our major business requirements were shown in that demo. It looks like that vendor just showed their generic package to us without even making configuration changes to show how it would work for our requirements. You two were supposed to meet with them and make sure that they demonstrated functionality that would work for our requirements!"

Wendy was beginning to get louder and more upset. Lynn tried to settle her down. "Wendy, let's talk about the specific requirements that were missing from..."

"Don't interrupt me!" she yelled. "All you have done is shuffle papers around for this whole project and look where we are!"

Lynn was stunned. She knew Wendy could be emotional at times but she had never seen her this upset. Wendy's last comment made her a little angry, but she could see that Wendy was taking out a lot of frustration on her and the firm. Lynn stopped and let her blow off some more steam before daring to say another word. When she did speak, she made sure to talk slowly and calmly and not pass any blame back to Wendy.

"I'm sorry the demo went wrong for you, but we want to make this right, Wendy. Can we go through the list of requirements and discuss how each one missed the mark?"

"Not a single one was discussed!" she bellowed.

"Well, let's go to the white board in the conference room and go through each one."

Lynn removed Wendy from her comfort zone by going to a neutral location. She also bought some time for her to cool down through the delay of moving the meeting. When they sat down and discussed it, Lynn learned that there were only three requirements that were misinterpreted by the vender that the directors were concerned about. Lynn suggested that they meet with the vendor to provide feedback on the requirements and ask them to provide a follow-up presentation to them and then to the three directors if the response was satisfactory. She also made a point to verify that the second vendor understood all of the requirements before their demo, which was scheduled for later in the week.

Wendy had calmed down significantly and was a bit embarrassed by her outburst. She said she would schedule a meeting with the directors to do a second review and thanked them for working out a solution.

Throughout the course of a project, despite the most detailed of plans, things go wrong. Based on the fees paid to consulting firms, clients sometimes have an expectation of perfection. Consultants also make good scapegoats when things go wrong. If the project sponsor is feeling heat, they may be likely to transfer that heat to the firm that is executing the project.

High tension and emotions can be contagious; one person gets upset and begins passing blame and the recipient ups the ante. In situations where clients get overly excited:

- Try to diffuse the situation rather than shooting back blame or insults; speak calmly in order to calm the client down.
- If possible, suggest a change of venue to a neutral location. The client may feel an exaggerated sense of power in his own office. Moving to a neutral conference room may calm him down.
- Get the client to focus on rational issues. Determine his specific issues.
- Approach it with a problem-solving attitude. Things may have gone wrong and mistakes may have been made, but the past can't be changed. Focus on what can be done to correct the situation.

Tip #30: Don't Flaunt Consulting Perks

Case Study:

HRS Consulting held their annual sales kick-off meeting the second week of January each year. This mandatory meeting for all managers and above was a three-day event in which the president presented the sales projections for the coming year, highlighted the successful projects from the past year, and provided breakout sessions for the Sales, Recruiting, and Delivery teams. It culminated on the last night with a formal dinner, after which awards were handed out to the high achievers in the group, including President's Club, the award of a four-day Caribbean vacation for all recipients who met or exceeded their sales and utilization numbers.

Parker was coming off an excellent year. His three projects put his utilization numbers well above his target. He also worked on the proposals for two of those projects and that allowed him to easily meet his sales goal. He was full of pride standing up on the stage when his name was called for President's Club. Aruba, here I come, he thought.

In mid-March he and his wife went to President's Club with the rest of the award recipients, the president, and his wife. They swam in the ocean, went parasailing, feasted like kings, and thoroughly enjoyed themselves for four straight days. On the last day, his boss presented him with his bonus check representing the equivalent of three months' salary. Parker was speechless.

They returned home late Sunday night and Parker needed to be back to work at the client site bright and early Monday morning. He did not have time to deposit his bonus check so he stuck it in his computer bag and went to work, intending to deposit it over his lunch break. Once at work, he loaded pictures of the trip from his phone to his laptop and showed them to some of his team members in the war room.

Later that day Parker was getting ready to go to lunch and pulled the bonus check out of his bag to take with him. He left it there while he ran to the bathroom. While he was gone, the consulting manager stepped in to ask Parker a question. He saw the pictures on Parker's screen saver and someone mentioned that it was from the trip he won from the firm. He looked on the desk and saw the amount on Parker's bonus check and was not sure whether to be more stunned at the amount or the fact that Parker had left it on the desk for everyone to see. He was going to remember this when the firm tried to raise their rates for their next project.

Consulting has its share of perks. The pay is often higher and there are bonuses and awards that often exceed what client employees receive. These are usually well-deserved benefits from a lot of hard work and long days. Clients often do not see the hard work as clearly as they see steep hourly rates they pay to the firms. The fact that the pay and benefits are deserved is irrelevant to most clients. That information is not the client's concern and should not be shared with them. Flaunting it in front of them, whether intentional or not, hurts the firm's credibility and negotiating power when it comes time to agree on the contract for the next project. It also reinforces the stereotype of a firm's aloofness in an environment where team building needs to be generated.

Tip #31: Consider Yourself a Leader, Let Others Use the Label

Case Study:
The dull roar in the conference room quieted a bit when Justin stood up to address them. When the last conversation ended, he began. "Welcome, everybody, to the project kick-off. My name is Justin and I'll be the project manager for this project."

He paused for dramatic effect. "I don't like to think of myself as a manager as much as a leader. I see this team as a great group of individuals that are even greater when they work together to reach our goal. I pledge to lead this team to accomplish our group goal and to help you all to achieve your personal goals as well."

Adam and Liz made eye contact with each other across the conference room table sharing the slightest hint of smiles. They had heard this speech from Justin in various forms several times before.

Justin continued, "On that note, I pledge to provide you with my leadership. If any of you ever need to sit down with someone for advice or just to talk some things over, my door is always open. You only need to stop in and ask."

Adam worked hard not to make eye contact with Liz anymore to avoid laughing. As Justin went on explaining the project and what the team could expect over the next few months, he sprinkled the word "leadership" in at least four more times by Adam's count. Adam thought "Leadership" could be a drinking game for the team. They could stop after work and have a drink for every time Justin mentioned the word. That's just too much drinking for one team, Adam reconsidered.

After the meeting, Liz and Adam met for lunch. "You know what's interesting?" Liz asked rhetorically, "Justin isn't that bad of a leader. He has confidence and is a pretty good decision maker. I just wish he knew how full of himself he sounds when he talks about it so much."

"Yeah," agreed Adam. "It's hard to take him seriously as a leader when he talks about it so much."

It's important for consultants at every level to be leaders. Leadership is comprised of many things. A leader makes confident, well-informed decisions. A leader adjusts his management style to the personality of the person he is dealing with. Above all, a leader knows how to earn the respect and credibility of the people he leads.

Boasting about what a great leader you are will erode that credibility. If someone is a great leader, other people will recognize that quality and begin calling him a leader. It should not be a self-appointed title.

Tip #32: Be Aware of the Effects of Your Public Image

Case Study:
As a senior manager at his large consulting firm, Bill had developed an expertise in healthcare consulting. He had served on projects for insurance companies and medical institutions over a span of several years. His current project was as project manager of an electronic medical records (EMR) system implementation at Carter Community Hospital.

As a conservative Republican, he took an active role in local politics. He had served on his local town board and had recently decided to run as a representative in his local precinct, which would be a part-time position allowing him to continue his career as a consultant.

As part of the election, he was subjected to a number of interviews from the local media. As he left a debate one evening, several reporters were present as he left the building. One reporter asked him about his opinions of healthcare reform, considering his background in healthcare consulting.

Bill replied in no uncertain terms, "I believe the healthcare reform laws will end up bankrupting our government as well as many of our healthcare institutions. If I'm elected, I will do whatever is in my power to reverse these laws."

His response was captured on camera by a local television station that aired it on the newscast that evening.

Stan Jennings, the chief executive officer of Carter Community Hospital, happened to be watching the news coverage. He called Bill into his office the next day.

"I saw you on the news last night and heard your comments regarding the healthcare laws."

Bill beamed, proud of his exposure. "Thank you," he responded. Although Stan was not one of his potential constituents, he believed he represented his client in his stand against the legislation.

"I have to tell you that I don't agree with your comments though."

Bill's face dropped. "Really, I'm surprised to hear that. Why not?"

"The healthcare reform laws have a lot of potential to give us headaches," said Stan. "It's part of the reason we have to pay you all of this money implementing the EMR system. But I--and most of our board--believe that in the long run, it will be good for us. There will be more people insured which will bring more people to our hospital. We also believe people will get medical attention earlier, which will give us a better chance of curing them, and doing it at a lower cost."

Bill was shocked. He had a lot of answers and statistics he could have shot back at Stan, but knew better than to get into what had become a political argument.

Stan informed Bill that he felt there was a conflict of interest with him serving in such a key role on the project. He had spoken with Bill's superiors and had requested a new project manager.

Bill disagreed but remained silent. He knew the decision had been made and there was nothing he could do to change it.

Consultants are human beings that have opinions about politics, religion, and many other topics which may be controversial to those who disagree with their opinions. It is important to keep any opinions that are unrelated to the execution of a consultant's job to himself.

A consultant should be just as cognizant of their public persona in case they take any type of public stand for or against any issue that may be considered controversial.

Whether you are running for local political office, attending a rally for or against gay rights, or drunkenly displaying private body parts on a video that goes viral, your actions may be witnessed by your client, causing anything from a strained relationship to a finished one.

Tip #33: Dress at or Above the Client's Standards

There was a time not too long ago when the suit and tie were standard attire in nearly any given business setting. It was easy for consultants to know how to dress at a client site. Today, dress codes at companies run the gamut from ultra-casual shorts and flip-flops to old-school suits and ties. These two extremes are fairly rare. It is more common to find a company with a business casual dress code, requiring a collared shirt and clean, pressed slacks for men. Attire for women is somewhat more flexible, but the standard rule for business casual is often no jeans. Some companies lighten up the dress code for Fridays, with business casual rules for Monday through Thursday and jeans allowed on Friday.

Regardless of a company's dress code, and their adaptations of the rules depending on the day or season, they all have internal employees that push the envelope for what is acceptable.

A rule of thumb for a consultant to follow is to dress at, or slightly above, the company's defined dress code. If business casual is the standard, make sure to always wear a collared shirt, and pressed dress slacks or khakis. If jeans are acceptable at the client site, it is a much more professional look to wear something a little less casual.

Some things to consider:

- Some clients want their consultants to blend in. If consultants wear suits when everyone else is wearing jeans, it can depict an air of elitism.
- Some consulting firms have strict rules against jeans--or denim of any kind--regardless of the client's dress code. It's best to be familiar with your firm's guidelines.

- Before making a visit to a client site, ask other members of the firm that have been on-site for their recommendations on attire.
- When in doubt about what is acceptable, watch what the client's executives wear and follow their lead.
- If you are unsure and there is no one to give you a suggestion, wear a suit. If they have a more casual dress code, you can always take the jacket and tie off for the remainder of the day.

Tip #34: Understand the Nuances of Client Perception

Case Study:
George tried not to respond when Scarlett walked into the meeting. He maintained his poker face even when he got around to her to give her status. Scarlett always seemed to miss the start of the meeting, but would arrive in time to give her own update. George always tried to keep the daily stand-up meeting to fifteen minutes or less.

After the meeting, George pulled Scarlett aside and asked to talk to her. They found an empty conference room and he maintained a serious tone. "I noticed that you've been arriving a little late for the daily stand-up meetings."

"Well I always get there in time to give my status," she said a bit flippantly.

"It's important for everyone to be there for the beginning so they can hear everyone's status. What if the first person that spoke had information that you needed to know about?" George asked.

"The client has people who come late, too. I'm not the only one," Scarlett replied even more defensively.

"I'm going to speak with them too. But it's hard for me to convince them of the importance of being there on time when my own team members don't follow the practice. As consultants, we need to set the example. But that's just a symptom of what I sense is a larger problem."

"What's that?" she asked, her guard going up a little more.

"It's the whole concept of client perception. Part of our job as consultants is to maintain a positive image for

101

the project. The other day when you referred to our requirements meeting as a 'big fiasco,' I don't think it reflected well on us."

"Well the meeting fell apart," Scarlett said. "I didn't say anything that they weren't already thinking."

"I agree," said George. "The meeting could have gone better. There was a lot of disarray at the end when they couldn't make a decision. But it does us no good to dwell on the negative. We need to maintain a good public image of the project."

Scarlett shrugged. "What was I supposed to say?"

"I would rather have you focus on the positive. Summarize what we accomplished. Then discuss what still needs to be done. But calling it a fiasco just ends up reinforcing the negative feeling."

"So in tomorrow's meeting do you want me to sugar-coat everything that's late?"

"No!" George replied, shaking his head. "I'm not asking you to sugar-coat anything. If something goes wrong, we just need to focus on how to fix and move forward."

Scarlett realized how serious George was and nodded.

A large component of consulting is not so much what is said, but how it is said and how it is perceived by the client. Stating things in negative terms or focusing on negative circumstances brands the consultant in the same way.

Even at a client that has a negative culture, joining in the pessimism will still have a negative reflection on the consultant.

Meetings go bad and projects get off track. The consultant is expected to remain positive without unnecessarily placating the situation.

When things go wrong, the focus should be on the next steps to take to solve the problem instead of dwelling on the problem or who is to blame.

Tip #35: Control Your Emotions

Case Study:

It had been a trying day for Mitch. His teenage son's grades had been dropping, causing a conference with his school counselor the night before.

Mitch and his wife had had some intense conversations with their son, but the two of them disagreed on how to deal with him. This resulted in heated debates between Mitch and his wife.

Things weren't going a whole lot better at work. Mitch's client project was currently two weeks behind. He had just come out of a meeting with the client manager who told him he was holding Mitch personally responsible for getting the project back on track. "Our end date is not moving, so you'd better figure something out," the manager told him as the meeting came to a close.

Mitch returned to his desk defeated. He was considering a number of options. He could have the team start working more hours, including mandatory weekends. He could also try to get additional consultants added to the project. Another option was to see if there was any functionality they could remove from the project to help them catch up.

All of the options had tradeoffs. He just needed some time to consider them all. Within minutes, he saw an e-mail come from the client manager addressed to the entire project team:

> *Effective immediately, the entire project team will work mandatory fifty-five-hour weeks, including weekends, until the project is back on track.*

Mitch was livid. It was his responsibility as the project lead to make that decision. Mitch immediately clicked the "Reply All" button and sent an e-mail of his own:

> *As project manager, the decision for how we get back on track with this project is mine and mine alone. Please disregard the previous e-mail until I announce my decision.*

That night, as Mitch walked out of the client's office building, he did so carrying a box with all of his personal items.

Every individual has highs and lows in life. At times, the lows can be so overwhelming that they negatively affect consulting responsibilities.

Consulting firms recruit people that are considered the best of the best. In addition to possessing a marketable industry skill set, exceptional interpersonal skills, and the ability to learn complex concepts quickly, they expect individuals to have perseverance, including the ability to deal with personal issues without them interfering in their consulting responsibilities.

When faced with highly emotional personal issues, combined with highly charged situations on the job that can tax his patience, a consultant has to maintain a professional demeanor.

It is imperative to put personal issues aside when on a client project. If personal issues prove to be overwhelming, most firms offer confidential, personal counseling services. A consultant would be well-advised to utilize those services if it would help him to maintain his wits on a project.

If you anticipate a long-term period of stress in your personal life that will affect your performance as a consultant, you may want to reconsider whether it is in your best interest to continue your career as a consultant.

Consulting can be a demanding career that taxes you with the number of hours and the level of stress and responsibility. If there is anything in your personal life that will keep you from being at the top of your game, a lower stress alternative may be best. It is common for people to take a break from consulting and re-enter a couple of years later. This may be a good time to take a respite to help get through a difficult time.

Tip #36: Anything You Do Can Affect Your Image with the Client

Case Study:
Neil and Larry were managers on a large consulting project at a Fortune Fifty manufacturing firm. Over the course of the project, they became good friends. They went to lunch regularly and had even shot a few rounds of golf together on weekends.

Their responsibilities on the project were closely related and on a daily basis, they met for coffee for about twenty minutes in the client's cafeteria. These were informal meetings where they would review the responsibilities for each others' teams and determine if there was any coordination they could do to get the best efficiency on the project.

The client manager was aware that Neil and Larry were close friends. He had joined them for lunch in the past and got along well with both of them. It bothered him, though, to see them sitting in the cafeteria every day as he walked through to get coffee. He knew they each billed out at more than two hundred dollars per hour and he felt he was paying them to chat over coffee. When he received the next invoice from their firm, he questioned them on how many of their hours he was billed for them to chat in the cafeteria. They were surprised by this question because they felt their morning meetings added value to the project and made them more efficient. From then on, they met in a conference room to hold a more formal daily meeting.

Despite what people may tell you about not worrying about what others think of you, it is absolutely

109

important in consulting. Client employees often feel threatened by consultants and may even view them with an air of distrust. Client managers are aware of the rates they pay for consultants' time and will view any impression of loafing on the job as a waste of their money. When consultants demonstrate any of their activities in too casual a manner, it can give the impression that the client is paying for activities with no value.

Meetings should give the impression of a meeting: They should be held at a desk or in a conference room. Coworkers often become friends, which is acceptable. Giving the impression that you are taking breaks with your friend rather than working gives the client reason to question billed hours.

Tip #37: Represent the Firm in Every Client Encounter

Case Study:
Virginia had been working on a consulting project at Garfield Corp., Inc. for the past six months. They had just surpassed a major milestone and she had been working some pretty long days. Now that things had settled down she needed to let loose a little. On Saturday night she went clubbing in the city with a few of her friends. They had been out for several hours and around midnight found themselves at Nitro, a popular nightclub.

While there, she bumped into Alex, one of the employees at Garfield Corp. She and Alex had been in several meetings together during the project and knew each other fairly well. They chatted for a few minutes and he bought her a drink. The conversation evolved to the project and they began discussing the work environment at Garfield Corp.

Virginia had had enough to drink to lower her inhibitions a bit too much. She began sharing her opinion of some of Alex's coworkers. Some of her critiques were harsher than others and Alex was a little embarrassed by her assessment of his peers. Then she began discussing some of the internal politics at her firm. She revealed that she thought her project manager was a jerk and that she didn't think he was very experienced. After a while, Alex politely ended the conversation, saying that he needed to join his friends.

The next day, Virginia remembered meeting Alex, but didn't remember much of the conversation. On Monday, her project manager called her into his office. He explained that it had been reported to him that she

111

had bad-mouthed some of the client employees. He told her that she was being removed from the project effective immediately and she was to report to the consulting office.

Virginia shakily packed up her personal items at her desk and returned to the office where she was given a lecture from the senior account manager on the potential harm she could have done to the firm by having such an indiscrete conversation with a client. News of her blunder got around the firm and it was difficult for her to get good project assignments in the future.

It can be common to develop loose lips when consultants bump into client personnel off-hours, or when they begin to develop a friendly relationship where they meet for lunch or drinks after work. Sometimes clients begin to share their own company gossip and a consultant feels the need to reciprocate. Good judgment needs to prevail.

Making disparaging comments about your firm or any of its employees hurts your firm's credibility. As a result, your credibility is also weakened.

When clients begin to ask specific questions, digging for a little dirt, don't accommodate them. If they push hard, a response such as, "I'm really not at liberty to discuss that kind of stuff," is appropriate.

If clients begin to criticize members of their own organization allow them to speak, but resist the urge to join in. As much as you may agree, and as much as they don't seem to mind, a situation in the future could cause them to turn on you and reveal your criticisms to your management.

Tip #38: Promote Yourself Within the Firm

Case Study:

As Pranitha finished her project, she was proud of her performance. She had learned so much over the past fourteen months. She spent six months in the first phase, gathering and documenting business requirements. The client was so impressed that they specifically requested that she be on the team for the implementation phase.

Randy, her project manager, wouldn't have had it any other way. He thought Pranitha was a born leader. She was organized, intelligent, and confident. People looked up to her and respected her opinion. She proved them all right during the implementation phase. The project was a huge success thanks in large part to her hard work.

As the project finished, Randy talked to the client about opportunities for additional projects. They were satisfied with the firm's work, but had no budget to start any additional projects.

Randy never spent any time on the bench when the project was over. He was immediately assigned as the project manager on another project that was starting up. He wanted to bring Pranitha with him but the rest of the team had already been assigned.

Pranitha went back to the office and waited for her next assignment. Every once in a while she called Randy to see if any positions opened up on his project, but he had nothing. She spent three weeks on the bench, watching her fellow bench mates get assigned to various projects. She couldn't figure out why, after doing such a great job, she couldn't get assigned to a project.

Doing a great job on a project is critical to being successful in consulting, but you also have to make sure that management in your own firm knows about it. You may create demand for your service capabilities at a client and with your own project manager. But, what happens if the client's funding runs out and they don't have another project to request you for? If the project manager has another project to manage, there is no guarantee there will be a position available for you with your skill set. Great consultants brand themselves with their clients and within their firm.

If you have a good track record for project delivery, make sure that your capabilities are known within the firm by the decision makers that staff new projects.

Meet as many top managers within the firm as possible. Introduce yourself at firm meetings and let them know who you are and what you have done within the firm.

Seek opportunities to speak at firm meetings. Most firms have periodic meetings, usually quarterly or semi-annually, to update their staff on new product offerings and to showcase a successful project that recently completed. This is an excellent opportunity to get public speaking experience and to get your name out within the firm.

Create a brand for yourself. Determine how you want to be known within the firm and live up to it. For example, if you want to be the guy that "will do whatever it takes to make the project a success," make that your trademark and you will eventually be known in that regard.

One caveat: Avoid using the hard sell while trying to market yourself. In an effort to become "the guy that will do whatever it takes to make a project a success," you could instead brand yourself as "the guy that keeps bugging the partners by bragging about himself while they're trying to get their work done."

Tip #39: Develop Multiple Complementary Skills

Case Study:

The IT team from Cass & Lemont Consulting had been brought in to review and assess the recommendations handed down from CLC's Strategy Assessment Team. The strategy assessment had been in the works for the past eight weeks. They interviewed various business units within the client and submitted a detailed recommendation for improvement. The main purpose of the report was to create pull-through business for the technical team to implement a solution. The "techies" were then brought in to implement the suggested IT initiatives.

As part of the IT team, Dmitri noticed that the members of the Strategy Assessment Team had difficulty understanding the technical details during the transition process. They were smart people. They all had MBAs and came from business backgrounds, but seemed to speak a different language than the IT team members.

He noticed a similar issue with the techies. Like Dmitri, they were all smart people with advanced technical degrees, but they didn't understand a lot of the business concepts that were discussed when they met with the Strategy Assessment Team.

As a result, Dmitri decided to get his MBA. He was accepted to a local university that had an evening and weekend program and was able to complete it within three years. By the time he was half-way through the program he noticed that he was more up to speed on a lot of the business concepts. He found he could work as a liaison between business and technical team members because he could speak both of their languages and act as a bridge to communication when there were breakdowns. This enhanced Dmitri's value within the company and increased the demand for him on future projects.

Developing multiple skills will go far in making yourself more in demand for new projects and reduce your bench time. Firms generally look for individuals that have a specific knowledge area in which they are deep, but with valuable complementary skills. Through your formal education, training, and experience you should develop an expertise in a skill that is in demand. Do your best to complement that skill with knowledge in related areas.

This doesn't need to include an expensive and time-consuming master's degree. IT knowledge can be complemented with subject matter expertise in accounting or finance. Business strategy knowledge can be complemented with an industry expertise in retail or publishing. Focus on related areas where there are projects that have a need for both skills.

Chapter 3 – Personal Branding

Think about the most popular brand names that you deal with on a day to day basis: Coca Cola, Nike, Apple. Think about the effort these and many other companies have put forth to brand themselves.

They've developed logos and slogans. But those are just components of their brands. Their brand is their reputation. If you love Apple products (and some people do), when you hear the name mentioned, you immediately get a good feeling thinking about the joy it brings you. If you absolutely hate Apple products (and some people do), you instantly develop negative feelings upon its mention.

Every human being is the same. Whether you think of the president of the United States or your Uncle Henry, they each have a brand in your mind. And that brand may vary based on who you ask.

Consultants each have a personal brand. If you work for a firm, your brand may be an extension of the firm's brand. But once you work with someone, you develop your own brand. It is important to develop a personal brand that is consistent with that of your firm. It is also important to develop your own distinct brand that people will recognize and think of in positive terms as soon as they hear your name.

Tip #40: Manage Social Media Appropriately

Case Study:

Chet was the project manager for a marketing strategy development project for Polk's Sporting Goods, a national retail sporting goods chain.

One Saturday morning, as Chet was preparing to take his son to a baseball game, his son showed him a broken strap on his catcher's helmet. Chet decided to make a stop at the local Polk's store to replace the strap.

It was a busy Saturday at the store and it took Chet a while to get a clerk's attention. When he finally got a clerk, the guy acted as though he was doing Chet a favor by waiting on him.

Chet showed him the helmet with the broken strap and asked if they carried replacements, the clerk replied tersely, "That won't do any good. That's just a cheap helmet. We sell some good ones over there."

Chet was angry and frustrated. He ended up taking his son to a competing sporting goods store to purchase a new strap.

When he dropped his son off at the game, he pulled out his smartphone, opened Twitter, and tweeted "Not shopping at #PolksSportingGoods anymore. Their employees are #rude."

Representatives at Polk's corporate office regularly monitored the major social media sites for mentions of their name. Chet's tweet was seen almost immediately and folks in their public relations department were notified.

One of the team members in PR recognized Chet's name and forwarded it to Charles Lee in marketing, who worked closely with Chet.

Monday morning on his way to the client site, Chet received a call from Bill, his manager at the firm. "Did you tweet something about Polk's Saturday?"

Chet's heart sank. He considered denying it, but he knew that his profile picture gave him away. "Uh... yes," he said reluctantly.

"I got a call from Charles Lee on Sunday. They want you off the project."

Chet resisted at first, but it fell on deaf ears with Bill. "Chet, Charles doesn't want you back on the project. Go directly to our office this morning. I'll get your personal items at Polk's and bring them to you."

A consultant should assume that anything he posts on any social media account is public and available to any client, regardless of the security set up on the account or pseudonyms under which the accounts are established.

This certainly applies to writing negative posts about a client. It also pertains to posts showing inappropriate or unprofessional behavior and controversial opinions.

Assume the client--and future clients--can read everything you publish. Post updates accordingly.

Embarrassing social media situations are a bad reflection on the consulting firm and can limit career advancement for the consultant.

Tip #41: Show Gratitude

Through the course of a consulting career, you will hopefully receive public accolades, awards, and promotions. These will primarily be based on your own performance; however it is rare to accomplish a major achievement without the help of a team.

When receiving a team award for which you are expected to make a public acceptance, always give thanks to the supporting team. If they are present, invite them with you to the stage or front of the room to be part of the acceptance. Within a week of acceptance, be sure to send a hand-written note of thanks to your direct manager and any other superiors who were instrumental in helping you with the achievement.

When you receive an individual award or promotion, a hand-written note to your immediate supervisor is also appropriate. It is never appropriate to send a gift, regardless of its value to a superior.

It is also important to show gratitude with a client on a day-to-day basis. Always thank the client team members when stopping for a question or when they send you information that they think would be helpful to you. It is amazing how far humility and gratitude will take you.

Tip #42: Make Yourself Indispensible

Case Study:

The Quick-Credit application development project for Pierce Finance, Inc. was far behind schedule. Business requirements were approved late and once approved, many new changes were added. The consultants with Choice Software Systems had created the appropriate change control forms to document the changes outside of the application's original scope, but the Pierce management team was adamant that the implementation date stay the same to coincide with the launch of their new product.

Logan was the lead developer on the project. She had spent many extra hours becoming familiar with all of the project's business requirements and all the changes to them. Everyone knew to go to her with questions on how the application should work.

Logan also had the most development experience on the team. Many of the junior developers turned to her for technical advice for some of the complex coding techniques.

Although everyone on the project worked long hours, Logan generally arrived before everyone at 7:00 AM and stayed until about 11:00 PM for nearly a three-week stretch. Her hotel was only two blocks from the client site and she saw nothing but the hotel and the client offices during that period.

After that Herculean effort, they were able to implement the application on time with only minor issues remaining to handle in post-production. When the project was over, her branch manager rewarded her with front row tickets to her favorite baseball team for the final game of the season.

But more than that, she developed a reputation with the client and with the firm as someone that could overcome whatever hurdles appeared to get the job done on time and done right.

As a consultant, your personal brand is critical. It is essential to have a specialty that makes people seek you out for advice. If you are also known as one that will go the extra mile and make sacrifices that others aren't willing to make, you will eventually brand yourself within the firm.

If the partners and project managers in your firm fight amongst themselves over you or if the client cringes whenever they think of losing you, you're on the right track.

Ways to brand yourself as indispensible include, but are not limited to, the following:

- **Come in early and stay late.** Nothing shows your commitment more than the willingness to work long hours. If you are on an hourly billing rate, it will be necessary to get the client's approval for the additional billing. It is also critical that the hours that you're working at the client, you're working *for* the client. Few things hurt your credibility with the client more than when they find you working on another client's work, or perusing the Internet on their dime.

- **Convince the client that they matter by putting their concerns first.** Every once in a while, a conflict of interest comes about. For example, if the client has asked you for a proposal to develop and implement a custom software system that stands to make your firm a lot of money in billable hours. If you know that there is a package on the market that would serve their needs, which they could purchase and implement for a fraction of the cost, what do you do?

If you put the client's interests first, you may lose out on potential revenue. But if you are half-way through the project when they learn of the package, that project may be the last one your firm does for that client. When you put their interests first, they will recognize it. They'll hire your firm for more projects in the future and may provide referrals to help your firm acquire additional clients.

- **Show the client that you are focused on their success.** Many consultants, in an interest to maintain a positive relationship with their client, assume the "no ruffled feathers" mode. Consider the scenario where the client is considering the purchase of extensive hardware to store their data on their premises. You may be aware of less expensive alternatives they could take. As one who has nothing to gain or lose in the hardware sale, you could allow them to make the purchase without ruffling their feathers by criticizing their judgment.

  If you are focused on their success, however, you need to speak up and let them know — diplomatically--that there are other options they could pursue that have potential to save them money. They may not always agree. But the client will know that you are focused on their success and will continue to listen to your suggestions.

Consulting rates are expensive. When economic situations get tight, clients have a tendency to start cutting consultants. If the client sees the consultant as indispensable, they will see that the value you provide to them is greater than the cost of your billing rate.

Tip #43: Share Your Knowledge

A consultant, by nature, shares his knowledge. Clients turn to consultants for advice to be shared. Knowledge is our product. But sharing of knowledge goes far beyond the day-to-day sharing with clients.

Knowledge should be shared within the firm so that consultants can learn each others' expertise. Many firms have knowledge management repositories that encourage people to share documents, processes, and best practices with each other. But sharing via face-to-face communication is much more effective.

Even the greenest consultant fresh out of college has some form of unique knowledge that can be shared with someone. Mentoring--whether formal or informal--is traditionally the role of older, more experienced workers sharing their years of accumulated knowledge with less experienced workers. But knowledge can be shared by younger people with more experienced coworkers.

Perhaps a young consultant has knowledge and experience with newer technologies that a more experienced worker is not familiar with. Sharing knowledge with anyone, regardless of the age of the learner, makes for a more efficient and more knowledgeable team.

Sharing of knowledge can be done in many forms:

- **One-on-one meetings.** Meeting individually, whether in formal, regularly scheduled sessions or on an as-needed basis when questions arise creates a forum for consultants to share knowledge with one another.
- **Lunch-and-learn sessions.** Allowing individuals at any level to host a lunch-and-learn session where

anyone interested in the chosen topic can bring his own lunch and hear someone give a presentation for one hour or less.

- **Lessons-learned sessions.** At the end of every consulting engagement, teams should assemble to review their lessons learned. Some firms make a practice of holding two separate sessions; one with client personnel present and one with only employees of the firm. A firm-only session allows them to speak more frankly about mistakes made and limitations in any of the firm's processes.
- **Publish your knowledge**. Using today's technology, it is easier than ever to create a blog on any subject in which you have some level of expertise. Many websites and online magazines welcome articles from people who have knowledge they want to share and can put it down in words that people can understand and learn from.

Chapter 4 – Expectation Setting

Imagine you are hiring a landscaping service to care for your lawn. You interview Baker Landscaping and explain to them that you would like the grass mowed and trimmed weekly, the flower beds weeded and the privet hedge trimmed every other week. The firm agrees to your terms and arranges to start the following Monday.

The next Monday as you arrive home from work, you notice that the grass is nicely manicured and the flower beds have been weeded. The privets remain untrimmed. Since you suggested that it be done every other week, you assume they will do it next week.

The following week, the lawn looks nice, the flower beds are weed-free, but the privets have still not been trimmed. A call to Baker results in the promise to trim them the next week. The next week rolls around, and the lawn has been mowed, but not trimmed, some weeds exist in the flower beds, but the privets have finally been nicely trimmed.

After calling Baker a second time, you learn that they were short-staffed due to an illness and they weren't able to complete the lawn trimming and weeding. They promise to make up for it the following week. On week four, they performed all tasks you had requested of them, however the privet trimming is uneven and they didn't remove all of the weeds in the flower bed.

You finally decide to change firms. Able Landscaping tells you that they can perform all of the responsibilities on your list and they begin the following Monday. Upon arriving home from work you find the lawn nicely mowed and trimmed. The privet hedge was nicely sculpted and the flower bed was weed-free. They have also used a blower to remove grass clippings from the driveway and sidewalks.

Weeks two and three bring the same results. On week four, as you arrive home, you find Able's truck is still parked in front of your house. A worker is raking privet leaves near the hedge and the other worker is preparing to start up the blower. When he sees you, he approaches and apologizes for still being there. They are short-handed today due to an illness so they are running late. As you inspect the yard, you see that all of the requested tasks have been attended to.

The above two scenarios are examples of one firm — Baker--underperforming to your expectations. Tasks were missed, excuses given, and promises made that were not fulfilled. The other firm — Able--exceeded expectations. They performed all tasks you hired them to do, cleaned up after themselves without being asked, and stayed late to get the project completed rather than making excuses.

In consulting, the service you provide is your only product. Customer satisfaction is obtained by setting the bar high and then providing service above the bar.

Tip #44: Exit Professionally

Case Study:

Naveen sat across from his account manager in the client's conference room and began to smile for the first time in quite a while. He was learning the details of the end of his assignment at this client.

The project had not gone well for him. He thought it would be a great opportunity to learn some new technologies, but he was assigned to a team that maintained an old system using old technologies.

On top of that, he just didn't get along with his client counterparts. He was assigned to two client employees that didn't accept him. They didn't think they needed help from an outside consultant and didn't include him in meetings and other critical information.

As a result, he was glad to be moving on. He was ready for a fresh start. His account manager informed him that this coming Friday would be his last day on the project. He would report to the consulting firm's offices the following Monday. For Naveen, Friday couldn't come soon enough.

He trudged through the week counting the minutes of each day. When Friday finally came, he ambled through the day, went to lunch with a few friends, and then cut out early.

The following Monday, when he couldn't be found, the client called Naveen's firm to find out where he was. Management at both the client and Naveen's firm were aware of him rolling off of the project, but both parties had relied on Naveen to inform his team and transfer whatever knowledge he had back to them prior to his exit.

There comes a time in every consulting project when the consultant leaves the project, normally known as "rolling off" the project.

Consultants are temporary workers. There is always the possibility that the client will ask for you to come back for another project, but at some point, you leave the client to work for another or to sit on the consulting "bench" waiting for reassignment.

Rolling off of a project can lead to mixed emotions. On one hand, one of the great things about consulting is the variety of experiences. This includes going to different clients, working with different teams and implementing a variety of solutions. Rolling off of a project is an opportunity to move on to another exciting opportunity.

On the other hand, if the consultant develops strong bonds with client personnel, leaving means cutting those ties. Today's communication and social media technology make it much easier to keep in touch with people, but nothing replaces seeing people in person every day.

Leaving a project should be more about the client than the consultant. It is important to make sure that you leave on good terms and the client is able to function in your absence.

So when a consultant leaves a project, the following tips should be considered.

Make sure the client identifies at least one contact to transfer your knowledge. Ensure that there is one contact person that you meet with to transfer your knowledge. It is best if this person is your replacement and will be fulfilling the same role you filled. It should at least be someone who has some familiarity with the project and will be available after you leave to answer questions anybody at the client may have.

Update the client's document repository. Make sure to leave behind any documentation that rightfully belongs to the client. If they have a standard repository, whether it's a proprietary system, SharePoint, or a simple shared drive on their network, copy whatever documents they may need in the future in a logical and appropriate location.

Document the transition. Leave behind a documented summary noting where key documents are stored and the final status of anything left undone. Share this document with any interested parties to ensure everyone has a good idea of the final status of anything you worked on.

Don't burn bridges. Regardless of the situation around leaving the client, there is nothing to be gained by destroying documents or relationships as you walk out the door. Always take the high road.

Say goodbye. If time allows, make sure to make the rounds and say goodbye to the people you worked with. It's also nice to send out a short e-mail to anyone you worked with. Tell them that you are moving on, that you've enjoyed your time working with them, and leave your contact information. Keep it brief. This is not a forum for emotional goodbyes or to opine on your philosophy of management.

Turn in all equipment, badges, and client property to the appropriate source. If the client gave you a laptop or any equipment to use while you were on-site, make sure to turn it back in to the department that issued it and that they verify that it is in acceptable shape. Turn your badge into the client manager you reported to or to security.

Connect with your client colleagues via LinkedIn. There isn't a more powerful way of keeping up with people than LinkedIn. This will insure you are accessible to them, and vice versa, for future networking opportunities.

Sometimes a consultant's roll-off is planned with plenty of time to prepare. In other situations it can be abruptly announced, effective immediately. There is not always time to leave things in perfect order. But doing everything in your power to reduce confusion after you leave will do the greatest good for the client and for your reputation as a consultant and a professional.

Tip #45: Under-Promise, Over-Deliver

Case Study:

When it came to efficient programming, Erica was a wiz at turning over assignments quickly and cleanly. She took pride at being able to write a program, test its results, and hand it over promptly. For Erica, it was an exciting challenge each time. She had worked for a small manufacturing company for about three years when she decided to give consulting a try.

For three years, she watched consultants get the more challenging programming assignments and it always seemed to take them forever. She could have completed their assignments in half the time. She thought they could, too, if they weren't charging by the hour.

Erica started with Masterson Consulting and was assigned to a client project where she would write applications for their e-commerce platform. The first assignment she was given was to create a complex application to interface with their client shopping cart software. Although the project was fairly complex she felt that the provided specifications and her skill were all she needed to complete it within five days. She submitted her estimate and got to work.

The task did prove to be challenging. The shopping cart software was not very well written and she ended up staying late a couple of days to meet the deadline. Things were going alright until day four when the shopping cart application server went down. She was stuck waiting for the outside vendor to fix the application for a full day. This put her a day behind. She let her manager know about the delay and was able to finish the work on day six. When she notified Suzanne, the designated business user that was supposed to test for her, she found out that Suzanne was on vacation for the next week. Suzanne had planned on testing on her last day before vacation. Because of the delay, she was unable to test as planned. Another day passed before they were able to identify another business user that could test, but he wouldn't be available for another three days.

In total, the assignment was handed over after two weeks--twice as long as her original estimate. The delays were caused by several events that were out of Erica's control, but since she estimated for the best-case scenario she had not allowed for any delays in the estimate.

One of the key aspects of setting client expectations is delivering to the client when you say you will. Downstream assignments are often dependent on the completion of your task, making delivery within the planned timeframe critical to the entire project timeline. Several considerations are critical when providing clients with an estimated delivery date:

- Consider how many external interfaces are required to complete the task. In Erica's case, she relied on the shopping cart server being up and running, and the business user being available for testing. Every external dependency adds risk to the task being delayed and should be taken into account.
- When providing an estimate, document your assumptions. If Erica had indicated to them that her assumptions included that the other application would be available for the duration of the task and

an alternative business user would be available in case the one assigned could not perform the duty, she would have set appropriate expectations for the client.

- Consider providing a range for best-case and worst-case scenarios. Erica could have estimated that this work would take anywhere from five to ten days depending on the assumptions above.
- Within reason, it's better to set the expectation that a task will take longer than you expect and beat the estimate, than to consistently be late on estimates.

Keep in mind that over-estimating can be just as damaging as under-estimating. It wastes time for implementation and often causes unnecessary gaps in the schedule and added expense to a project. The goal in estimating is to come as close as possible to enable accurate planning across an entire project.

Tip #46: Verify Every Client-Facing Deliverable

Case Study:

The offshore facility finally submitted their functional requirements document and e-mailed it to Sarah. It was 9:00 PM local time. She was exhausted, hungry, and tired of waiting for something she had planned on getting around lunch time. She had also promised the client that the document would be e-mailed to them by the time they arrived at work the next day. When she made the promise, there seemed to be plenty of time. Now she was at the eleventh hour. She forwarded the document to the four client recipients and powered down her PC. Another long day in the books.

The next morning at 8:20 Sarah was powering up her PC. Doug, the client lead on the project, called her in hysterics. "Did you read this document?"

"No, I just got in and was going to review it this morning."

"All I see is jumbled up text and special characters! I've got a meeting in ten minutes where we were supposed to discuss this document. I've got nothing to talk about. I'm going to have to cancel the meeting at the last minute. How much are we paying you guys to deliver crap like this?"

What a lovely way to start the day, Sarah thought. As her PC came up, she opened the document. Sure enough, it looked like twelve pages of hieroglyphics. "Doug, I don't know what happened here. They sent it late last night. I'll try to find out if they can fix it and resend it."

"Well that will be too late for my meeting. You guys are really going to have to bump up the quality here if you expect to get any more projects from us."

"I understand," replied Sarah. She was desperate to end the conversation as well as the scolding.

Deliverables are sent to clients in many forms. Word processing applications, such as Microsoft Word, have various versions and releases and sometimes files get corrupted during electronic transfer. Any deliverable that is presented to a client, whether it is a Word document, PowerPoint presentation, or computer program, should go through a formalized proofread by another responsible party, or testing in the case of a computer program. Sending untested or unverified deliverables to a client creates a reputation of sloppiness and unprofessionalism.

If Sarah had taken the time to open the document to proofread it, she would have seen that it was in an unreadable form. She could have taken measures to repair the document herself or call the offshore facility to make corrections and resend it, regardless of how late she had to stay.

When submitting a deliverable to a client:

- Spell check isn't enough. Read the document thoroughly and verify correct grammar and word usage.
- Confirm that each paragraph has a main idea.
- Make sure every sentence is complete.
- Most firms have standards of uniformity for deliverables. Standards may include font style and size, branding of the firm's logo on the cover sheet, and information in the headers and footers. Make yourself familiar with these standards and follow them. Create a checklist of things to verify.

- Review either the printed format, or a "print view," on the computer screen. Some views don't show the header and footer, which may have old text from a copied template.
- If the document has a table of contents, verify that the page numbers are accurate for each entry.
- Have a peer review the document, if possible. A second set of eyes can often catch things that an author will miss even after several reviews.

In most cases, it is better to miss a deadline than to submit unprofessional work.

Tip #47: Trust but Verify

Case Study:

The new Accounts Receivable Processing System (ARPS) was complex and required input from several key users. In addition to weekly team meetings to gather business requirements, Cory met individually with a number of people in the business that had minor involvement in the process. He felt this was the best way to get their input while saving them the time of attending long team sessions.

He met with Jan for a one-on-one session. She gave him a lot of information regarding the workflow. She explained how receivables were generated by the distribution area, when they sent the product out the door, and how her team processed the receivables and sent it on to the credit department. Jan used to work in credit so she provided a lot of detail about how they process it once her team sent it on. Cory thought it was a great session and it filled in a lot of information gaps for him.

Two weeks later, he submitted his completed business requirements document to the client team for approval. After reviewing it, Nancy, the credit manager, sent him an e-mail stating that their process had been documented incorrectly. She said the documented workflow was not at all how they process orders. He called Nancy right away and explained that this was the way Jan had described it to him.

"Jan hasn't worked in Credit in four years," Nancy said. "That may be how they did it when she worked here, but we have a much different process now."

Cory scheduled a meeting with Nancy for the following Monday and resubmitted the corrected document, causing his project milestone to be a week late.

When getting information from individual client employees, they don't always know things as well as they think. The main purpose of organizing cross-functional teams is to allow each person in the process to explain their role in a chain of events so that each participant can confirm or refute the information. It often comes out in these sessions that two groups perform redundant activities because neither group knew what the other was doing.

There can be efficiencies to meeting with individuals if they have only a small part in a process. That information should be presented to the core team for validation or reviewed with another group or individual that has a touch point to the process in order to get the story from another viewpoint. If Cory had met with Nancy in addition to Jan, he would have gotten the process right the first time, saving him both the embarrassment and the project delay by submitting incorrect documentation.

Tip #48: Know the Project Purpose and Scope

Case Study:
Mary Beth was a business analyst working on a project at Madison Manufacturing. One morning a manager with Madison came by to ask her to run some queries on the database so they could do some data analysis. Mary Beth spent four hours running the queries and assisting them with the analysis.

On Monday, she submitted her status report to her project manager with an entry describing her additional task. The project manager questioned her on it and explained to Mary Beth that the task was not part of the agreed upon scope for the project. By the contract, they may have trouble billing the client for the work. The work also put Mary Beth behind schedule on her project tasks that were due for the week.

When a consultant is assigned to a project the project manager should clearly define the scope of the project and the specific assignments the consultant will be responsible for. If this is not made clear, the consultant should seek clarification about the information and ask if there is a project charter. Almost every project has a project charter that spells out the reason the project is being executed and the parameters around how it will be performed. This includes a detailed description of what will and will not be done.

If a client approaches a consultant and asks them to perform a task that they are not sure is in scope, the project manager or another manager should be notified to make a determination. How strictly this is enforced depends on the amount of time the task takes--is it ten minutes or several hours--and the type of contract the project is under. A time and materials (T&M) contract specifies that the consulting firm can charge for all hours burned. Scope is not watched as closely in this situation.

A fixed bid contract specifies that the client will pay only a fixed amount for a specific scope of work. Project scope is defined much more tightly and followed more closely on fixed bid contracts.

Tip #49: Drop Everything--The Client Needs You

Case Study:

Getting up at 4:00 in the morning and taking the three and a half hour drive to Indianapolis made Karl cranky and irritable. He had been called down to fix some coding errors left by the implementation team that he worked with. All of the other team members had been assigned to new projects, so Karl was nominated to fix the bugs. He spent the whole day at Taylor Legal Services writing and fixing computer code. After grabbing some dinner, he finally checked into his room at 10:00 PM. Collapsing into the stiff bed, he slept restlessly and woke before the alarm at 6:45 the next morning. Still tired, he showered and checked out of the hotel for one more day of code fixes.

He had things working, tested, and signed off by the client by about 3:00 PM and was ready to take the long drive back to Chicago. Then, his cell phone rang. Another one of his clients in Indianapolis, Fillmore Produce, had some questions and heard he was in town. They wanted him to stop in to discuss some issues they were having with the Record Tracking System he had helped to install several months ago. He explained that it was too late in the day for him to stop because he had the long drive back home. He would call them in the morning.

The next morning Karl reported to the office intending to call his client at Fillmore Produce. There was a note on his desk from his manager to stop in and see him.

When he got to his manager's office, she didn't greet him with her usual warm smile. "I received a call from Maggie Richardson at Fillmore Produce yesterday afternoon. She was a little upset that you didn't stop by while you were in town."

"I was just about to give her a call," Karl explained. "I was dead tired and needed to get on the road. I didn't want to get home at 10:00 at night."

Karl's manager looked at him, disappointed, and explained, "Karl, Fillmore paid us $350,000 for that software implementation and there is potential for us to do a lot more work with them. We need to treat them, and all of our clients, with more respect than that. If they had wanted us to drive down there and talk to them, we would figure out a way to do it. You were across town and refused to see them. That's unacceptable. If you couldn't fit it into the day yesterday, you should have gotten a hotel room for another night and stopped by in the morning."

Clients are the lifeblood of consulting. They pay the bills that pay the paychecks and bonuses. As such, client service must be a top priority. Consulting is a competitive industry. If a client doesn't receive good service from one firm, they will take their business elsewhere.

Consultants need to have a client service attitude, responding promptly to any client request and striving to satisfy them with every contact. Consultants that make lemonade out of lemons and treat client problems as opportunities are the ones that usually get chances for follow-on work. Difficult clients should also be treated as a challenge. Setting a goal to please the seemingly "unpleasable" client will not only impress them, but the decision makers that surround them.

Chapter 5 – Communication

One of the most critical skills that a consulting firm looks for in the hiring process is a candidate's ability to communicate. Few questions are ever asked about communication. Instead, every interaction a candidate has with a firm is a test of her ability to communicate.

Firms look for consultants that have excellent written, verbal, and non- verbal communication skills:

- Does she communicate well under pressure situations?
- Can he speak and write a full sentence without grammatical errors?
- Does she think before she speaks?
- Does he understand his audience and tailor his communication accordingly?

Consultants may have a lot of skills that would make them good candidates for consulting, but good communication skills are the glue that brings all of those skills together and make an all-round quality consultant.

Tip #50: Speak When You Are Angry and You Will Make the Greatest Speech You Will Ever Regret

Case Study:

Cleveland Office Supplies was the toughest client Stephanie ever had to work with. She had been paired up with Brad, the director of purchasing, who was the most demanding person she had met yet in her career. She felt that she could do nothing right for him. He criticized every deliverable she presented and complained even when she submitted assignments on time.

After this morning's weekly status meeting, she typed up the meeting minutes and sent them out to all of the attendees. Six minutes after she clicked the "Send" button, Brad replied to her with a "Reply All," with copies to her project manager and his boss, the chief marketing officer:

> *Stephanie*
>
> *Your notes state that I said that we should benchmark competing firms on their marketing strategies. That's not what I said. My statement was that we should see if there is benchmark information on the industry that we can compare to our approach. Please correct the meeting notes and resubmit.*
>
> *Brad*

Stephanie was steamed. Not only had she written what he said verbatim, she didn't understand why he had to copy the whole damned world on such a subtle difference in perception. She immediately fired back a "Reply All" of her own:

> Brad:
>
> *I distinctly remember what you said in the meeting and documented it as such. If you would like to change what you said, I'd be happy to include a retraction in an updated version of the notes!!*
>
> Stephanie

A few minutes later, Stephanie's project manager was at her desk asking to speak to her in the conference room.

Sometimes clients seem to go out of their way to make a consultant's life difficult. Perhaps they resent outsiders coming in to tell them how to do their business or they have decided that beating up on consultants is cheaper than therapy. A thick skin can be a consultant's greatest asset, but clients can agitate even the most callous consultants.

When a tough client or intense situation causes you to get emotional the best thing to do is remove yourself from the situation. If this occurs in a meeting, request that you take a ten-minute break or suggest tabling the discussion until you can gather more information.

When you receive a flaming e-mail like the one sent to Stephanie, the best thing to do is walk away. Take a walk, breathe deeply, and, most importantly, think about the most appropriate and professional way to handle the situation. Regardless of how rude or unwarranted a client's treatment is, the worst thing you can do is retaliate. With some difficult people that is exactly what they are trying to accomplish. Do not give them the satisfaction. Although falling on your sword may seem like a painful option, in the long run it is much less painful than evening the score.

After taking some time to calm down, a more appropriate response may have been the following:

Brad:

When taking meeting notes, I try to get them as accurately as possible. If I misunderstood your statement, I apologize. Please see the corrected meeting minutes attached.

Stephanie

Tip #51: Don't Use "Consultant-Speak" To Impress

Case Study:

Jenna was planning for her first steering committee meeting. She was a little intimidated thinking about presenting to three directors, two vice presidents, and the chief information officer for the client. She only had three slides in the presentation to deliver on their analysis approach; she wanted to make a good impression and wanted to prove her credibility. She did not want to come off looking stupid in front of such high-level people.

As the team entered the room and sat down, she started her presentation. "Thanks for attending our presentation. My name is Jenna Arnett. I'm a senior project manager with Oak Street Partners and I'd like to give you an overview of our two-phased analysis approach.

"In this paradigm, we start out with a five-thousand-foot view of your current state scenario. This will give us enough information to develop a straw man and identify any low-hanging fruit that we can grab for a quick kill."

Jenna continued talking with all eyes on her.

"That will allow us to obtain a quick understanding of the system and identify some fast benefits. At the end of the day, however, that won't be enough. We will need to circle back and do a deep dive into the current state analysis. Then we will bring in Scott Sanchez. He is our resident rock star on this subject matter. He has amazing bandwidth and adds a lot of innovation to this process. He will run our visioning sessions and get us to think outside of the box to identify our future state blueprint.

We will rely heavily on the synergies created between our team and yours to keep us on plan and make sure we don't boil the ocean. We want everything to have a positive cost-benefit for your business model.

"Once the future state vision is complete, we will perform a gap analysis to identify how we are going to get from point A to point B. We will do our due diligence to identify the best practices for your industry to implement a system that gives you the best bang for your buck."

Jenna paused and looked at everyone.

Consultants often get the impression that they need to impress the clients with overused "consultant-ese" dialogue filled with clever catch phrases and jargon. Perhaps they figure if they can't dazzle with their brilliance, they can baffle them with their bullshit. This type of talk, however, comes off as boorish and condescending. Speak to clients in clear, straight-to-the-point statements to inform them rather than to impress them. If the presentation is technical, avoid use of technical jargon or acronyms, even if it's part of your everyday conversation.

Tip #52: Don't Be Condescending to the Client

Case Study:
When the enterprise software implementation team needed an expert on data warehousing, Mark, the project manager, requested Art to come out for a day and perform an assessment of their current application and provide some recommendations for improvement. Art had several years of experience and was known throughout the consulting firm as the data warehousing guru.

For a day and half, Art met with members of the data warehousing team and the business manager in charge of data analysis. Then he and Mark met with Jill Garner, the client manager, to present his findings. Art began explaining some of the weaknesses in their existing application and promoting some of the more advanced technologies that were available. He then suggested some more sophisticated approaches that Jill's company could use. Jill was always a little suspect of advice from consultants and wanted to determine whether her current applications, while maybe not the state of the art, were sufficient for their needs. She began asking questions during Art's presentation to get a clearer picture.

Art was on a roll and did not like being interrupted. "Jill, what I'm saying is very important to your organization. You need to stop talking and listen to me." He continued on, criticizing Jill's applications, calling them dinosaurs compared to what was currently available.

Jill kept a cool exterior, but was steaming like a runaway locomotive internally. She felt like she was paying Art a lot of money to criticize her company's applications and to tell her to shut up. When Art finished, Jill thanked him and told him she would review his report and get back to him. After Art left, she pulled Mark aside and told him that she never wanted Art on-site again.

Organizations hire consulting firms because they are looking for the advice of experts. They know that their current processes and applications need improvements.

People usually become consultants because they have a special skill either from training, experience, or both. That is what lends to their authority and credibility to offer business or technical advice. As an expert, you are expected to know more about a subject than the client. How you present that to them is the key to success:

- When doing an assessment of a client's current state, present it in non-critical terms. If it is inefficient explain that there are ways that it can be improved. Do not criticize the system as bad or antiquated.

- When discussing improvements, explain them in terms of benefit to the client rather than simply that they are better or newer than their existing systems.

- There is the old maxim that you have two ears and only one mouth, so you should listen twice as much as you talk. That may be hard when giving a presentation, but when a client has questions they should be given every opportunity to ask them. If they do not apply to the conversation, suggest that the question be tabled until you can follow up with them later. Presenting to a client should be more of a conversation than a lecture. Involve them and give them credibility and respect.

160

Tip #53: Speak with a Purpose

Case Study:
The weekly status meetings were the worst hour of the week for Kathy. She had been managing the creative design project for three months. It was going well and was on time and within budget. The firm's sales rep, Dan, came on-site once a week for the status meetings. She didn't understand why he felt he was needed for the weekly meetings. She would update the management team on the accomplishments of the past week and any existing risks or issues that needed management's attention. When Jesse, the client manager, would make a point, Dan would usually follow with, "I agree with Jesse," or "That's an excellent point." Sometimes he would paraphrase what the client said without adding any new ideas.

Dan's presence only increased the length of the meeting and frustrated Kathy in the process. Kathy wondered if Dan really thought he was adding value with the comments he made.

Regardless of whether you are in a meeting or a one-on-one conversation, determine your role in the interchange and put thought into each statement that you make in order to maximize its value. Are you there to be informed or to contribute to the discussion? People whose purpose in a conversation is to be informed should generally remain quiet and take in the information. Questions should be asked when clarification is necessary.

Instead, people feel the need to have their voices heard and make benign statements in order to be noticed rather than appear as a wallflower. This not only wastes the time of everyone involved, but reduces one's credibility when adding "white noise" statements that add no value.

Every statement you make is a reflection on the firm. Making intelligent statements and asking pertinent questions increases credibility for you and your firm.

Tip #54: Convey Confidence

Case Study:

McKinley Glass Products needed guidance on their tax strategy. Reliable Tax Consulting was contracted to analyze how the new tax guidelines would affect them and to make recommendations on changes that would reduce their tax liability.

Margo had four years of tax experience in her previous company, but was new to tax consulting. She had only been on board with Reliable for a month and this was her first client gig. She felt intimidated, not only by her peers within the firm, who had much more consulting experience, but also by the client's employees. Two months ago, she was doing the same thing that they do. Now they are suddenly looking to her for advice. She had been hired by Reliable because she knew the tax code backward and forward, but that did not help her confidence. She felt like a fraud, charging them the fees that Reliable was charging. She knew that any minute they could expose her shortcomings.

Margo used her fear as an incentive to work harder and she loved doing the heads-down tax research. It took her mind off of her insecurities and allowed her to avoid interaction with anyone at the client site.

After two weeks of studying the client's tax strategy and reviewing the tax code, she came up with a strategy that would save McKinley Glass Products an estimated $2.4 million in taxes over a three-year period. She and the Reliable team prepared their final strategy to give to the vice president of finance. Antonio, the project manager, assigned Margo to give the presentation.

She dreaded the prospect of presenting to the vice president and her staff. She was up the entire night before, worrying about the types of questions that could be asked and how she might not be prepared. At the presentation, she hemmed and hawed and was visibly nervous. The vice president did have some tough questions about the recommendation. Although Margo was able to answer each of the questions, her nerves gave the impression that she didn't believe what she was saying.

After the presentation, the vice president pulled Antonio into her office. "Margo didn't seem to have much confidence in your proposal. Do you really think we can save $2.4 million with this approach?"

"Absolutely," Antonio replied. "Margo knows this tax code thoroughly. She's a little inexperienced in public speaking, but this approach is rock solid."

"I don't know" said the vice president. "I'm going to have another firm review this idea and give me a second opinion on it."

A key factor of success in consulting is self-confidence. The client needs to believe in you. As a consultant, you are brought on to a client's site for your expertise to either define or resolve a problem.

But having expertise is only part of the show. You need to be able to come up with the answers and present them in a convincing way that makes the client buy in and believe in your recommendation. Salesmanship is a major part of consulting. You are always selling the firm's capabilities, but you must also sell your ideas to avoid the client questioning your ideas, and as a result, the firm's ultimate product.

Confidence can also be taken to an extreme. Arrogantly telling a client what to do, regardless of how strong you feel, will not work either. The client is paying for your advice, but is not committed to following it. Much as a doctor can tell a patient to watch his diet and exercise and give sound arguments for making these lifestyle changes, the ultimate decision still lies within the hands of the patient. The same applies to consulting.

Tip #55: Have a Sense of Humor, Use It Wisely

Case Study:

Jason was well liked on his team because he was always happy. His smile and his laugh were contagious and he always seemed to have a funny story to perk up the room. Jason's manager, Phil liked having him on his projects because he could add flavor to the most boring meetings and make them just a little more bearable. Jason also had a lot of experience in marketing strategy and had an excellent creative mind when it came to brainstorming.

Phil invited Jason to an important client meeting that the client's chief executive officer, Mr. Majors, planned to attend. They were going to discuss the findings of their marketing study and try to get their foot in the door for another project that was coming up for consideration. Phil knew that Jason had some great ideas and wanted to get him in front of Mr. Majors.

Mr. Majors was a stern-faced gentleman of about sixty. While the dress code at the company was business casual, Mr. Majors always wore a button-down shirt with a sport jacket. He walked in the conference room at exactly ten o'clock and sat down saying, "I have a hard stop at ten-thirty for a conference call with Europe."

"Wow," Jason said. "How do you get all of Europe to call in at the same time?"

There was a nervous chuckle from some of the meeting participants, but Mr. Majors just looked at him and said, "The call is with our directors in our European office." It seemed he seriously thought that Jason believed every resident of Europe would be on the call.

Phil sensed that Mr. Majors wasn't in the mood for humor and began passing out the meeting agendas.

"Since we only have thirty minutes, I think we should jump right into this." He began a serious discussion of their findings. Every few minutes, Jason jumped in with a humorous comment, which Mr. Majors did not laugh at or acknowledge. When the thirty minutes was over, Mr. Majors thanked Phil and left unceremoniously for his conference call.

The other client employees shuffled out of the conference room leaving Phil and Jason alone. This gave Phil an opportunity to talk to Jason in private. "Jason, I want to talk to you about your joking around."

"Yeah, that Majors guy doesn't seem to have much of a sense of humor, does he?" Jason replied.

"Really, I didn't think you noticed. You should have figured out from his response to your first joke that he either didn't appreciate your sense of humor or wasn't in the mood for it. If you had stopped then and there, it would have been okay, but you didn't seem to get the hint. That kind of behavior hurts our credibility."

Everybody enjoys a good laugh once in a while. A sense of humor can add some spice and break the tedium of a long and boring meeting. But like spices in food, everyone has his own tastes and too much can spoil a good recipe:

- Be aware of your audience and try to gauge the audience's receptiveness to humor. Back off and assume a serious approach if they don't seem to appreciate it.
- What is funny to one person can be offensive to another. Be careful not to joke about anything that might be considered controversial or sensitive.

168

- One or two humorous comments sprinkled sporadically throughout a meeting can lighten the environment and can even make a meeting more productive. You still need to remember that a meeting is not a party and there is no consulting award for "Life of the Meeting."

Adding too much or inappropriate humor can put your credibility in question, particularly if the client thinks you are not taking your billable hours seriously. By now you realize what that does--it hurts the firm's chances of additional work.

Tip #56: Prepare Your Message Before Making a Call

Case Study:

Deeply engrossed in typing her client presentation, Jordan came across some information that she wanted to verify. She quickly picked up the phone to call Jenny, the client manager. As the phone rang, she continued typing. She barely heard the call go to voice mail and when she heard the beep, she suddenly realized she was supposed to talk. She had planned on Jenny answering the phone and hadn't considered that she would have to leave a message. Jordan was concentrating so much on her typing that for a split second she forgot who she was calling and why.

"Oh...uh...yeah...um...oh yeah, Jenny. I'm working on tomorrow's presentation and I had a question. Let's see...it was on this page somewhere. Oh, yeah, uh...here it is." She continued to ramble on for a few seconds until she remembered her question and finally got it out, but not before sounding like a complete idiot.

When approaching anyone via telephone--client, manager, or peer--with a question, stop and take thirty seconds to:

- Formulate the question. Make sure you can efficiently introduce whatever facts are necessary for her to understand the issue and answer the question.
- Jot down some of the main points of the question you are going to ask. This will allow you to better organize your thoughts.

171

- Verify that you are asking the appropriate person. If the subject is outside of his expertise, stop to think about who might be a better person to ask.
- Consider that she may not answer the phone. Prepare a statement that would be appropriate for a succinct voice-mail message. This will help you to frame your question even if she answers the phone.
- If the question is too complex to leave as a voice mail, simply ask him to return your call. Tell him what the question is regarding so he can be prepared to answer it.

Tip #57: Reply to Messages and Meeting Invitations Within One Business Day

Case Study:
The hectic pace of the project and its aggressive deadlines were getting to Diana. It seemed that she barely finished one assignment for the project and the next deadline was looming. It was everything she could do to attend all of her meetings and then get her assignments done. She was perpetually behind on her e-mails.

Sue, the client manager, was located at another building within the client's corporate campus. She had been trying to meet with Diana for two days. She had scheduled a meeting with Diana through Outlook, but got no response. She sent another e-mail and tried calling, but got her voice mail. None of the messages were returned. Sue was frustrated and assumed Diana was ignoring her request. She finally went for a walk to the building where Diana worked and hunted her down. When she finally tracked her down, she explained that she had been trying to schedule a meeting with her for days and wondered why she was disregarding her messages.

Diana apologized and said she hadn't been ignoring her. She just hadn't gotten to her e-mails and was weighed down by the volume she had received.

Regardless of the number of e-mails and voice mails you receive, it is important to reply to all messages from the client within one business day. Most business cultures are e-mail happy. It is so easy to shoot off an e-mail and when multiple people are addressed, it is an invitation to start a long thread where everyone needs to get in their two cents. The volume can be overwhelming.

At least once per day set time aside to review e-mails.

Within the e-mail application create folders of meaningful categories to store e-mails after you have read and acted on them appropriately. This allows you to maintain a history of your e-mails while getting them out of your inbox.

If there are a lot of e-mails in the inbox, sort the e-mails by subject line. This will arrange e-mail threads together. Read the last e-mail in the thread from the bottom up. This will give you the whole thread in one e-mail. Once you have read the full thread, reply as necessary and move all of the e-mails with that subject line to the appropriate folder.

Look for meeting invitations so you can reply to them in time for the person scheduling the meeting to reschedule if you are unable to attend. If you decline a meeting invitation, provide a reason and suggest other times when you can attend. It may also be appropriate to suggest an alternative person who can fill in for you.

Most e-mail programs have tools that allow you to color code e-mails. It might be helpful to show e-mails in red from important senders. Another color can be used for e-mails addressed specifically to you, versus a group of recipients.

Tip #58: Write Professional E-mails

In the old days of business communication, before everything was electronic, there was the inter-office memo. This was a semi-formal note, typed on paper, with paper copies distributed to all recipients. When computers gained prevalence and were networked together, the memo evolved to the e-mail. Today, e-mail serves as a replacement for the formal memo and a host of other formal and informal inter-office communications.

Since e-mail is used for so much informal communication people tend to use it informally for work. The result is that what should be professional communication can appear very unprofessional. When sending business e-mails, especially to clients, certain standards should be followed.

Address the recipient every time. You would not just start talking without saying "hello" during a phone call. The same goes for e-mail. Do not start an e-mail by just typing. Always address the recipient to whom you are e-mailing. This starts the e-mail with a much softer tone and doesn't come off with a blunt statement or question. This is especially important if the e-mail is copied to a group of people. Many copied recipients don't realize that it's for information purposes and may be confused thinking the e-mail is directly to them. Not everyone reads the header information to see that others are addressed. If the e-mail is to a group, try to address them as a group such as "Implementation Team Members." Additionally, when a group is being addressed and a question is being asked, it's best to state to which person the question is directed.

Proofread every e-mail before you hit "send." It is important, even in informal communications such as e-mail, to look and sound professional and intelligent enough to justify your rates. Some misspelled words exist in a dictionary and are not caught. Additionally, incorrectly using same-sounding words (homophones) such as *there, their* or *they're* and *to, too* or *two,* give the impression that you never mastered the English language.

If the e-mail is to an important group of recipients, consider typing the text in Microsoft Word, which usually has more robust editing features than most e-mail programs. This doesn't eliminate the need to proofread your text.

Finally, stop to think about the point of view of the recipient. Determine the purpose of the e-mail and make sure it is made clear in the first one or two sentences. It can be frustrating to get an e-mail where a question is asked and you have no idea what the sender is talking about.

Avoid texting abbreviations. Texting is so commonplace in today's world that it has taken a life of its own. Evolving from cell phone keypads that only had ten keys, each number represented three or four alphabetic letters, requiring users to enter the number multiple times in order to enter the desired letter. Because this was cumbersome, users naturally developed shortcuts to enable fewer keystrokes to get the point across. By the time cell phones evolved to smart phones with full QWERTY keypads, the practice had become a permanent fixture of our informal culture and is the norm for much of our typed communication.

E-mailing friends and e-mailing business clients are two completely separate forms of communication. Regardless of the ability of the recipient to read texting shorthand, it is not a professional way to communicate in a business e-mail. E-mails to individuals get forwarded to larger audiences. If the e-mail eventually gets to the client who is the decision maker and they read the full thread it will be a poor reflection on you, the consultant. Casual forms of communication should not be used in a business e-mail.

NO YELLING. Many business people get more than two hundred e-mails per day. In an environment like this, there is a tendency to go to extreme measures to get someone's attention. One common approach is to type a full e-mail, including the subject line, in ALL CAPITAL LETTERS. This is the written form of yelling at someone in full voice.

It may be effective in getting someone's attention, but is even more effective at annoying a client. If you need to get someone's attention to respond to an e-mail, begin the subject line with "Urgent: Response Requested" or some text that will stick out in the Inbox queue to increase the odds of being seen and responded to. Similarly, many e-mail programs allow the sender to assign priority to a message. These approaches should be used sparingly to ensure that they are effective.

Have a call to action. When an issue is identified, it is the consultant's responsibility to drive it to resolution.

When sending an e-mail to resolve an issue:

- Address the e-mail directly to the person you want to resolve it. Copy other team members who need to be aware of the exchange.

- If you want the recipient to do something, make that part of the opening statement rather than the last part of the e-mail.
- State specifically what you want the recipient(s) to do: "Paul, since you are the inventory management representative on the team, would you please investigate this process?"
- If there are many details to provide, consider listing them in a separate attachment.
- Provide a timeframe that you would like the recipient(s) to follow up. Rather than setting it as a firm deadline, state when you would like to have the information, asking for feedback if it will take longer: "I would like to have this resolved by our meeting on Friday, if possible. If this is not possible, please let me know when you think you might have this information."
- If you are only informing someone of a situation, state that this is just for informational purposes: "FYI, I will investigate this and hope to have feedback for you in Friday's meeting."
- If you have more than one question, consider sending separate e-mails. This will avoid getting only one answer and having to follow up. If you have a number of questions, it may be best to meet face-to-face.

Tip #59: The Client's E-mail System Is for Client Business

Case Study

Emma and Steffen were each given a company e-mail account within their first week on the project at Harding Manufacturing. It was convenient because its address book held all of the client employees, so they didn't have to enter the e-mail addresses of their client teammates in their firm e-mail system's address book.

They worked on opposite ends of the third floor so it was convenient to e-mail each other to send documents or a quick note without switching over to their firm's e-mail system. As the project wore on they both developed a disdain for the client manager, Sean King. He seemed aloof and condescending. He often tried to embarrass people in front of a group. In one meeting with the client team, King was in rare form and made a point of embarrassing Steffen. Steffen didn't have an answer for his question, so he gave the advantages and disadvantages of each option presented. King publicly berated him. "Aren't you supposed to be the expert?" he asked sarcastically.

After the meeting, they went back to their desks and Emma sent a quick e-mail to Steffen asking what he thought of King's latest shenanigan. Steffen went off on him. His obscenity laden response slammed King for his behavior. Referring to some past instances where they expensed some non-business lunches to the client, he suggested they do it again just to get back at King.

Unbeknownst to them, Harding Manufacturing had an obscenity monitor on their e-mail system. Among other things, it monitored for any foul language as a defense against harassment. Steffen's e-mail generated an incidence report which was routed directly to Sean King's attention. After reading the report, King requested a full review of their e-mail activity since the project's inception. The report showed several instances of the two slamming client management and employees. It also revealed the exchange of firm-specific information which divulged billing rates and profit margins for the firm on this project and for other projects at other clients.

King scheduled a meeting with the firm's account manager, which included representatives from Harding's legal counsel. Later that week, Harding Manufacturing officially severed ties with Emma and Steffen's firm. The firm swiftly followed suit with Emma and Steffen.

Every company has their own policy for e-mail usage. Some monitor usage closely while some do not monitor it at all. As a consultant, it is best to assume that all e-mail usage at the client is monitored and make a practice of only doing client-related business on client resources. Personal communication should be done on personal devices on personal time away from clients as much as possible to avoid giving anyone at the client the impression that you are doing non-client activities on their dime. Confidential firm business should only be conducted on the firm's secured systems.

Tip #60: Forward E-mails with Care

Case Study:
Mallory was pleased to extend an offer to Vanessa for the title of senior consultant. She was sure Vanessa's experience and personality would be a great addition to her consulting team. She sent an e-mail to Nate in Human Resources asking him to extend the offer for an annual salary of $95,500. This was the top end of her budget, but she knew she could staff her on billable projects immediately and that her previous consulting experience would require little training.

Nate replied back asking a few questions regarding when she wanted Vanessa to start and in which orientation activities she would like Vanessa involved. Mallory provided Nate with the appropriate information and a couple days later, he replied, asking who Mallory would like to have assigned as Vanessa's mentor. Mallory wanted to assign Shawn, but wanted to check with her to ensure she had enough flexibility in her schedule. She forwarded the e-mail to Shawn asking her about her ability to serve in this capacity.

Shawn made a habit of reading the full threads of e-mails she received, regardless of how late in the thread she was included. In this thread she saw Vanessa's starting salary. She had interviewed Vanessa and given feedback that she didn't have strong enough technical skills to fulfill this role. Additionally, a month ago, Shawn had requested a raise from her current $92,000 and was turned down with the reason that they did not have enough money in the budget. Now she was unintentionally informed that they had ample budget for Vanessa, but not Shawn. She considered approaching Mallory about this, but didn't feel she would get anywhere with it. Within two months, Shawn had found a new position with a competing consulting firm and had moved on.

Take care when forwarding an e-mail to make sure that the historical information in the thread does not contain sensitive information that should not be shared. In this case, Mallory may have had a legitimate reason to pay Vanessa a higher salary than Shawn. Allowing Shawn to learn her salary, however, not only created a poor morale situation, but exposed Vanessa's confidential salary information to a peer. It also lost Mallory an employee. Always make certain historical information in the thread doesn't contain confidential or incriminating information. This is particularly critical when forwarding e-mails to clients.

Tip #61: Control Runaway E-mail Threads

Case Study:

Malcolm's requirements document came to a standstill when he came to a point of decision. He needed input from the user community to complete the document. He sent an e-mail to six key users asking them to provide the input he needed to enable him to move forward.

Over the course of the next two days, all the recipients sent "reply all" messages with their input. Two of the recipients added additional people for their input. Eventually, the single e-mail had snaked out to four separate threads in which sixteen different people were participating.

In addition, people had removed some of the addressees from the original e-mail so redundant points were being made in the various threads. Malcolm was getting confused over which thread was which. Besides redundancies there was also conflicting information. Everybody involved in the e-mail thread was confused by the end.

E-mail threads tend to evolve. Sometimes the original subject line is completely unrelated to the actual topic of what the message morphs into. The subject line even gets changed at times as the thread grows. At some point, Malcolm should have stopped the madness and scheduled a meeting with the knowledge providers, asking them to invite whomever they felt could add value to the conversation. As this progressed, time was wasted with inconsistent and redundant information that would have been more efficiently communicated with all of the necessary people in one room.

Chapter 6: Meetings

Meetings are the ultimate necessary evil in business. In my career, I've seen more time wasted in meetings than by any other activity. Some people come to a meeting with a different objective than that of the meeting. That is when meetings get out of control and valuable time is spent on topics other than the purpose of the meeting.

The fully loaded cost of an employee is the consolidated cost to a company for her salary and benefits, such as vacation and insurance, plus the overhead costs--office space, heating, cleaning, etc. Some companies have algorithms of varying complexity to determine this value. The general rule of thumb for an average employee's fully loaded cost is approximately $100 per hour. Multiply that times the number of people in attendance, times the number of hours of the meeting to give a good idea of the true cost of a meeting.

There are legitimate purposes for meetings as long as they are run efficiently and are focused on their objective. When clients pay their consultants based on the hour they want to see them pay attention to efficiency want to see them pay attention to efficiency.

Tip #62: Promptness Is a Sign of Respect

Whether you are the host of a meeting or an attendee, one of the most effective ways to show your disrespect and unprofessionalism is to show up late. This also clearly demonstrates to your client and peer group your total disregard for their time.

If you wish to show your client some respect, set a target to arrive at every meeting one to two minutes before its scheduled start time. Few meetings start exactly on time. Others may be late, there are technical difficulties, and sometimes a prior meeting in the same conference room runs long. None of these are excuses for showing up to a meeting after its scheduled time.

If you schedule the meeting, it is usually necessary to arrive several minutes early to verify that there is enough room and seating for all attendees. If any additional resources, such as an easel pad, markers, or a computer and projector, are required these should all be set up and ready to use at the meeting start time.

Everyone runs late on one occasion or another. A previous meeting runs late, traffic is heavier than expected, or the president of the company stops you and asks a long-winded question on your way to the meeting. This should be the exception and only occur in rare circumstances. When it does happen extend an appropriate apology and little harm will be done. When it is habitual, regardless of the excuse or apology, you will develop a reputation for tardiness which can result in a loss of credibility and respect from the client.

Tip #63: Have an Agenda

Case Study:

The client team members called her "Meandering Meeting" Martha because of the way she ran--or didn't run--meetings. When Martha scheduled a meeting she usually had a general idea of what she wanted to discuss. During the meeting she always seemed to get sidetracked.

Martha would start out her meetings with small talk about the latest story she heard on the news. Then she would talk a little business. After that, she would wing it, seeing what others in the group reminded her of and ask whatever questions seemed to be nagging at her. In one meeting with ten attendees, she spent fifteen minutes discussing an issue with one person while the other meeting participants bided their time.

People had given up asking her in advance what would be discussed in a meeting because it always ended up being different by the time the meeting started.

Meetings should be held only when necessary and should be run efficiently to avoid wasting valuable time and money. One way to ensure an efficiently run meeting is to have an agenda.

The agenda should contain the following items:
- Date, time, and location of the meeting
- List of all invitees
- Objective of the meeting
- Bulleted list of each topic to be discussed and who is expected to provide input to the topic

When you schedule a meeting, send the agenda to each invitee at least one day in advance of the meeting, if possible. Bring hard copies to the meeting.

Facilitate the meeting to the agenda by keeping meeting attendees on topic. If a topic takes much longer than expected or the discussion meanders to additional topics bring the focus back to the agenda. You can suggest that it be tabled for a separate conversation.

Tip #64: Only Invite Necessary People

Every minute wasted in a meeting is multiplied by the number of attendees. Additionally, the more attendees in a meeting the more difficult it is to keep order and come to a resolution. People sometimes feel the need to speak in a meeting to justify their attendance. This often adds unnecessary time and discussion to a meeting.

The primary purposes for attending a meeting are to:

- Provide information to the meeting attendees.
- Obtain information from the meeting attendees.
- Exchange input to resolve an issue.

There are often political implications for determining attendees for a meeting. If someone is not invited they may feel they are being left out of the loop. If someone is unnecessarily invited, they may be upset that an hour or more of their valuable time was wasted.

When establishing a list of invitees to a meeting:

- Determine who is required for the meeting based on their need to provide or to be provided information.
- If someone is not necessary to the meeting, but may be interested, invite them as an optional attendee.
- If an individual only needs to be kept in the loop, ask them ahead of time if they would like to be invited or if the published meeting minutes will suffice.
- When suggesting to someone that they are not needed in a meeting, make it clear to them that your purpose is not to keep them out of a meeting but rather to assist them in making the best use of their time.

Tip #65: Be Prepared to Take Notes

In a utopian world, every meeting would have an agenda, a facilitator, and a defined scribe for taking the meeting minutes. A consultant should always make sure these responsibilities have been arranged prior to a meeting that he organizes. This is often not in one's control when attending a meeting organized by someone else. Regardless of who schedules a meeting, a consultant should be prepared to take notes in some manner. Bringing a pen and pad of paper or a laptop allows you to:

- Be the impromptu scribe of the meeting in the absence of one.
- Take your own notes to compare to those of the formal note taker in case they miss critical information.
- Take note of any action items assigned to you in the meeting.
- Show to the client that you are prepared for the meeting.

Walking into a meeting empty handed gives the impression that you plan on being an observer and that you aren't prepared to even write down your own action items. When that happens, you will end up borrowing something to write with.

Do not rely on a mobile phone for note taking. When taking notes on a phone, the client doesn't know if you are texting a friend, checking baseball scores, or actually taking notes.

Tip #66: Anticipate Questions the Client Will Ask

Case Study:

Danielle's to-do list was long and she had to squeeze her many tasks between four meetings throughout the day. She was good at time management and prided herself on scratching off most, if not all, of the high-priority items from her list every day.

She had her weekly status meeting with client management at 2:00 and had to break the news to them that they were a week behind on the project. She planned to work through lunch and then attend a 1:00 meeting with the users to clarify some requirements. The requirements meeting went long and she had to leave at 2:00 to rush to the status meeting. She had prepared her agendas in advance and began facilitating the meeting.

When she got to the part about the project delay, she explained that the reason was due to new issues presented by the user community. She provided detail about the issues and explained why it would take a week of time out of the project timeline.

As she went to move on, the client manager began asking questions about the issues. She wanted to know who introduced the issues and when. She asked why the issues hadn't been escalated to management if they were going to cause such a significant delay. Most importantly, she wanted to know what alternatives Danielle had considered prior to extending the project.

Danielle was caught off-guard. Because she was so busy, she hadn't considered the questions and concerns the client would have. She didn't have answers for many of the client's questions and gave the impression that she was unprepared for the meeting.

Meetings require preparation time not just to assemble and print agendas, but also to consider how each agenda item will be received by the meeting participants.

Consider how familiar each bullet point is to the attendees; do they already know what you will be covering or is it new information? Reflect on how this information will affect their ability to do their job and complete their assigned tasks.

Few people like to be surprised with bad news in a meeting in front of several people. When possible, provide bad news in advance to avoid blind-siding people in a public setting.

Tip #67: Come to Meetings Prepared

Case Study:
Brett spent a week working on the PowerPoint presentation for his project's kickoff meeting. When the day came for the meeting, he was feeling confident that he'd make a good first impression with the client.

Five minutes before the meeting, he grabbed his laptop and went to pick up the projector he reserved at the client's office services desk. When he arrived, he saw a note that said, "Back in 5 minutes." He started to panic. He wondered how many minutes ago the note was placed there. The attendant returned after about two minutes, but it seemed like an eternity. She handed him the projector and he bolted for the meeting room.

Brett found several of the meeting attendees already there. He introduced himself as he started up his laptop and connected it to the projector. He had some trouble getting the image to project and had to reboot the computer again. Brett noticed some of the meeting participants looking at their watches.

When he finally got through all of the technical issues, the kickoff meeting got kicked off fifteen minutes late. This was not the first impression that Brett had in mind.

A meeting that gets off on the wrong foot is difficult to salvage. When facilitating or organizing a meeting, proper preparation is imperative.
- Double check to verify that a meeting room is available and has ample room for all attendees.

- If a computer and/or projector will be used verify their availability and allow extra time for set up and resolution of any issues that can occur.
- When possible, have backup technology available in case anything malfunctions.
- If documents are to be displayed via projector, have hard copies as backup handouts in case of technology failures.
- Printers and copy machines generally jam during their most urgent need. Make copies of handouts well ahead of the meeting to avoid stressful moments with the printer two minutes before a scheduled meeting.

Tip #68: Turn Off Your Phone

Few people understand how critical meeting time is. It is important to focus on the meeting's objective and avoid disruptions as much as possible. One of the most common disruptions to a meeting is the ringing of a mobile phone. Even worse is answering a call or a text. Paying attention to your phone or anything not pertaining to the meeting shows a lack of respect to the other attendees.

There are legitimate reasons for answering one's phone in a meeting--an expectant father waiting for news or someone on call for system outages. In these cases, the meeting attendees should be informed that you will be monitoring for specific messages and that you will try not to be disruptive to the meeting. Outside of these types of critical situations, mobile phones should be turned off or silenced so that all attendees can focus on the meeting and not be distracted by ringing or vibrating phones.

Tip #69: Introduce the Meeting

Unless a meeting is held on a regular basis with the same people, such as a weekly status meeting, the facilitator should begin by stating the purpose of the meeting and its objective--what you hope to accomplish by the end of the meeting. If there is anyone unfamiliar with anyone else in the meeting, it may be appropriate to go around the table to allow everyone to introduce themselves and the department in which they work. This allows the audience to understand everyone's knowledge base in the meeting and who they may direct their questions to, should they arise.

Meetings often go off course as people get off topic. While introducing the purpose and objective of a meeting will not guarantee that people will stick to the topic at hand, it increases the odds and allows the facilitator to more easily bring people back on track.

Tip #70: Sharpen Your Presentation Skills

Regardless of whether you are an entry-level consultant or have several years of experience, you will be expected to speak in front of a group of people. There are various levels of comfort in public speaking. Some people relish the attention and look forward to opportunities to speak to a group. Others get uncomfortable even answering a question in front of a group.

Effectively standing up in front of a group of people to present is a skill that requires practice and experience. Few people are naturals at it. Like any skill, the more you do it, the better and more confident you become at it.

In order to develop your presentation skills:

- Practice your presentation. If it is a prepared speech, practice in front of the mirror. If the meeting room is available, go to the room where the presentation will be given to get more familiar with the surroundings. Make sure to speak out loud to simulate the actual speech as closely as possible.

- Videotape your presentation so you can view it and critique areas that you need to improve upon. Do your research. Be certain that you are familiar with the topic you will be presenting. Prepare answers to potential questions that could be asked and rebuttals to alternative views.

- When presenting by PowerPoint or some form of hand-out, do not read to your audience. Summarize what they are reading and add to the written information with additional information that supports it.

- If you find yourself nervous at the beginning focus on relaxing. Straighten your posture and take a couple of deep breaths. You may be anxious to start talking, but the audience will not notice a four- or five-second "relaxation delay" before you speak. It will make an amazing difference for you.

- Start out by breaking the ice. Make a casual comment, perhaps complimenting the group for being on time for such an early meeting, or simply thanking them for their attendance. This allows you to develop a rapport and get a comfort level with the crowd before getting to the important information of your presentation.
- Consider joining Toastmasters International (www.toastmasters.org), a non-profit educational organization that teaches public speaking and leadership skills. There are thousands of local chapters all over the world. They provide opportunities for experience in giving presentations and many other skills to help professionals succeed.

Tip #71: Stay Awake

Case Study:
Kyle had the boys over to his place for Monday Night Football. He enjoyed a few beers and they all celebrated when his team won the game in overtime. He didn't get to bed until way past midnight and was dragging most of the next day.

At lunch he needed something to coat his stomach and went out for a big heavy meal. By the time he got to his 1:30 meeting, he was feeling pretty drowsy. This was a requirements gathering session in which he was the scribe. About thirty minutes into the session, he had totally spaced out and was half-asleep. The team was discussing an issue and had a question about what they had decided earlier in the meeting.

One of the client team members asked Kyle what he had in his notes about the issue. Kyle wasn't asleep, but he might as well have been. He had few notes on his pad and had no idea what the client was talking about.

Some business meetings can be long and boring. It is often difficult to stay focused without a good night's sleep. A short night or a heavy meal can make staying awake a challenge. Caffeine and power drinks will only go so far in substituting for a lack of sleep.

Napping or spacing out in a client meeting is an excellent way to be asked to leave a project. Clients rarely have a lot of tolerance for consultants who nap on their dime. In order to stay focused always make it habit to:

- Get a good night's sleep and avoid excessive alcohol on work nights.

- Eat a lighter than usual lunch if you will be attending a mid-afternoon meeting.
- Drink lots of water throughout the day and during the meeting.
- Take notes to force yourself to focus on the discussion--even if you are not the scribe.
- Sit up. Sitting back and getting comfortable will make you sleepier.
- Get out of your seat, if possible, if you feel yourself losing focus. Standing up will help get your blood flowing. You can stand up against a wall or step out to use the washroom and splash some water on your face. It may give you the boost you need to stay focused.

Tip #72: Maintain Control of Your Meeting

Case Study:

Abby was facilitating a requirements gathering meeting with a cross-functional team of client employees. She felt the meeting was going well, but needed input from everyone. Kelli from Accounting hadn't said a word. She had spoken with her one-on-one before and hadn't gotten the impression that she was shy.

She felt part of the problem was Jarrod. Jarrod represented Marketing and seemed to have an opinion on everything. He acted as though Marketing was the only department in the company and seemed to have an opinion on every issue, whether it affected his department or not. Some of his comments didn't even make any sense. Abby wondered if he just liked hearing his own voice.

As the meeting came to a close, she felt they had spent too much time talking about Marketing's needs and not enough on Accounting.

There are timid people who are scared of their own shadow in meetings. On the flip side, there are those that will say something stupid or irrelevant in front of a group of people. Some just get flustered and curl up under the pressure. What does this tell you? You find every type of personality imaginable in a meeting. If you are running the meeting you need to keep all those personalities under control and focused on your agenda.

As a facilitator, it is important to control both extremes. If people have not spoken and you know they have knowledge of the topic at hand, ask them their thoughts and encourage them to participate. They may be too scared to speak or simply have trouble getting the attention of the team.

On the other end of the spectrum, the meeting hijackers need to be reined in. There are diplomatic ways to table discussion of off-topic issues. You can also state that you'd like to get as many opinions as possible to encourage others to speak. This, of course, must be tempered by the political power of the person speaking.

Most importantly, in order to prevent team participants from being too timid or too obnoxious, it's best to lead by example. Speak when you have something to say, and only then.

Tip #73: Keep Phone Attendees Aware

It is common for meetings to have remote attendees on speakerphone. If anyone is attending the meeting via conference call, it is appropriate to announce all people in the room. If participants join the room after the introduction, their presence should be announced as soon as there is a break in the discussion.

In addition, any activity taking place in the meeting that a remote participant cannot see should be described. For example, if a diagram is being discussed from a handout or information is on a whiteboard, all participants should be aware to assist them in following the conversation. When possible, handouts should be sent electronically to remote meeting attendees. While the document is being discussed, make sure they know what page is being discussed whenever possible. You may want to consider video conferencing options such as Skype (www.skype.com), WebEx (www.WebEx.com) and Go to Meeting (www.GoToMeeting.com) if this is practical.

One other helpful note about remote attendees you should know. This is more and more common as work-from-home arrangements gain popularity. If you are the one calling in, do so with as little background noise as possible. Many calls from home-based workers have background sounds of dogs barking, babies crying, and lawn mowers bellowing outside. Flushing toilets have even been known to occur. Background noises can't always be avoided when working from home, but reducing them as much as possible will create fewer distractions and present a more professional appearance. The mute button can be your friend.

Tip #74: Track Action Items and Issues

When meeting discussions generate issues that need to be resolved, make sure the issues are documented and that the person responsible for its resolution is identified.

Action items should be tracked as well. Make sure that the responsible parties are identified. Published meeting minutes should list all open issues and action items, along with assigned parties and target dates, when applicable.

If there is a follow-up meeting, all meeting attendees with responsibilities should be contacted by the facilitator within two days of the follow-up meeting to gently remind them of their responsibilities. If no follow-up meeting is held, the facilitator is responsible to inquire on each item and verify that all issues are resolved, all action items are completed, and that everything is appropriately documented.

Tip #75: Publish Meeting Minutes

Although there is an assigned scribe responsible for taking notes in a meeting, the facilitator is responsible for meeting minutes being published to all attendees and any other interested parties. Meeting minutes should closely follow the bullet points of the agenda and discuss only pertinent discussion items and any decisions made regarding each topic.

It is standard practice to list all invitees, identifying who in the list was in attendance. Discretion should be used in exposing anyone who was absent for political purposes.

Additionally, the meeting purpose and/or objective should be stated along with action items and issues. Minutes should reflect a general summary of the discussion with the final decisions rather than a transcript of what every person said.

When sending the meeting minutes to the team, request feedback from the team for any additions or corrections within a specific time, usually one to two business days.

Chapter 7 – Sales

Many consulting firms have a dedicated sales staff to sell the firm's services. In most firms, however, every consultant, from entry level to the firm's chief executive officer, has some responsibility for sales. The key ingredient in sales is the establishment of a relationship. Entry- and lower-level consultants are rarely exposed to decision makers at the client, but every activity they are involved in is a reflection of the firm and can negatively or positively affect the chances of the firm getting future projects.

As you start out in consulting, billable hours will be your primary focus. Entry-level consultants are usually held responsible for eight-five to ninety percent utilization, allowing for vacation and administration time. At this level, responsibility for sales will be negligible. Sales credit may be given if a consultant assisted on a winning proposal or if her performance on a project contributed to follow-on work. As consultants move up the ladder, their utilization percentage expectations are gradually reduced as their responsibility for sales increases. A senior consultant may be responsible for eighty to eighty-five percent utilization, but will be expected to begin developing relationships at her assigned clients in order to influence add-on project sales.

Tip #76: Know Your Firm's Service Offerings

Most firms have a single-page overview of their solution portfolio summarizing the products and services they provide. It's often available on the firm's website. Becoming familiar with this information provides sales opportunities in a number of situations.

When trying to spot potential project opportunities on the client site, a thorough understanding of the firm's capabilities will give you a better idea of what type of client issues you are looking for.

Casual relationships on the golf course and dinner parties often present opportunities. As friends discuss issues they have at work, sound knowledge of your firm's offerings will give you opportunities to make suggestions and possibly create new leads for your firm.

While unassigned to a project (on the bench), there are two goals:

- Get assigned to a project
- Get assigned to a proposal team in order to acquire sales credit and get assigned to that project

A solid understanding of your firm's offerings will increase your chances of getting assigned to a proposal team. In turn, it increases your odds of increasing your sales and utilization numbers.

Tip #77: Know the Expectation for Sales at Your Level

Case Study:
As Bailey's first day for her new job at Colfax Consulting approached she began to get anxious. It didn't help that she had lunch with her father's friend Tanya, who had several years of consulting experience.

Tanya explained to her that the ability to sell consulting services was of utmost importance for moving up the ranks in consulting. Bailey was suddenly filled with apprehension.

She had never considered herself as a sales person. In fact, she studied engineering instead of business in part to avoid getting put into a career focused on sales. Now she was told that selling would be a major factor in her success. She considered backing out and starting the interview process all over again.

Instead, she decided to tough it out. When she arrived for her first day of work, after filling out what seemed like endless insurance and tax forms, she attended an orientation class with the twelve other new hires in her group.

The orientation covered several areas including the history of the firm, their dress code, and the firm's vacation and paid time off policy.

At the end of the day there was no mention of her responsibility to sell or any training on how to sell. She was, however, assigned a mentor named Alyssa. The next day she met with Alyssa and asked her about being responsible for selling. Alyssa explained to her that since she was just starting out, she would be held responsible for little to no sales quotas.

"Your biggest responsibility at your entry level is to make sure you keep your utilization high," Alyssa explained.

"My utilization? What's that?"

"Your billable hours," Alyssa replied. "You want to be billable about ninety percent of the time. That's all you need to focus on. You won't be held responsible for sales until later in your career."

Suddenly Bailey felt much better knowing she wouldn't need to start selling consulting services this early in her career. That night as she lay in bed, she ran the conversation back in her head. Suddenly a thought struck her. How do I keep my utilization at ninety percent?

Although most firms have evaluation metrics for soft skills such as learning and communication, sales and utilization are the most important at most consulting firms.

A successful firm needs people that are capable of selling projects to clients as well as people who can serve on those projects in order for the firm to bill the client for the revenue.

Selling consulting services is not like selling hot dogs at a roadside stand. Selling services successfully is the result of developing long-term relationships.

As the general career progression goes, early in one's consulting career, a consultant is responsible almost entirely for her utilization. A consultant can influence that by providing service so superior that she will be in demand for a new project before finishing the current one.

As the consultant begins moving up the consulting career ladder, she begins being held responsible for progressively fewer utilization hours and more selling.

At higher ranks within the firm, such as senior manager or partner, consultants become more responsible for finding leads and being rainmakers within the firm than for billing hours.

While lower-level consultants should focus on remaining billable, they can begin networking to develop relationships in the following ways:

Client employees at their same level. A consultant who is just a few years out of college will very likely be teamed up with client employees at a similar stage in their careers. Developing a good relationship with your client peers can be the basis of a long-term relationship for many years. Whether that person stays at the client or moves on to other companies, as they advance in their careers, they become decision makers who are more apt to call someone they know for services they need.

Client executives. Even consultants who are in the early years of their careers can gain access to executives at a client. That can occur through meetings in which they both attend or through word of mouth within the client. When a consultant excels at what he does, clients will often talk. And word can get up to the top executives who may request you for the next project.

Join trade or professional organizations. By joining an organization that is related by area of expertise, a consultant can begin networking and making contacts that can eventually lead to business opportunities.

Deliver excellence. Providing excellent client service is a great way to get a client to hire your firm for follow-on services. Clients usually have many projects in their backlog. They have a wide array of choices in consulting firms to help them implement those projects. If you serve on a project and impress the client, they will be more likely to ask for your firm--and you--back for the next project.

Identify opportunities for additional work. Consultants working close to the front lines at the client have access to more information than they usually realize. Client employee peers sometimes get pulled away to resolve issues unrelated to the project. If you become aware of a recurring issue that could be resolved by your firm, mention it to your manager as a potential opportunity. Keep in mind that every opportunity you identify will not translate into a sale. Don't get discouraged. It may take five, six, maybe even ten suggestions until it actually pans out.

Even if none of your ideas result in a sale, it shows to your management that you are focused on helping the client solve problems and identifying new opportunities for the firm.

Keep your eyes and ears open for the client's pain points. Though you may develop relationships with their management level, they aren't going to spoon-feed new business to you. Listen, ask questions, and recognize areas where the client could use your firm's help. Do it with a goal of helping the client rather than racking up sales.

Know your firm's service offerings. If you are familiar with the capabilities your firm has outside of your own specialty, you will be better prepared to recognize where your firm can help the client resolve their issues.

Work on sales proposals. When you are unassigned, or "on the bench," try to find out if any proposal teams are working on a new client proposal. Volunteering for the team will establish you as someone who is willing to help out. It may also provide you with enough familiarity of the project issues to get you assigned to it if the proposal wins.

Tip #78: Network Effectively

The Internet and particularly Web 2.0 tools have facilitated social media such as Facebook, Twitter, and LinkedIn, just to mention a few. These tools have made it easier than ever to develop a vast network of friends and business acquaintances. They are effective in helping a person to avoid losing contact, as well.

In the pre-Internet days when people met prospective business associates, they would exchange business cards or phone numbers. Businesspeople collected stacks of business cards and carried day planners full of hand-written phone numbers. If the business associate changed her contact information, it was difficult to update everyone in her network and people often lost touch over time. The Internet tools available today allow contacts to stay connected.

Whether you are collecting business cards or developing a large contact list on a site such as LinkedIn, the overriding principle has not changed: Meet as many people as possible and develop business relationships with them.

To some degree this is a numbers game and quantity is important. It is more important, however, to develop quality contacts that will remember you if you need to reach out to them.

There are many opportunities to meet people in business and personal settings. Some suggestions include:

- Meetings held with prospective clients
- Dinner meetings with colleagues
- Join a professional organization that has monthly meetings and social activities
- Strike up a conversation with someone at lunch

- Join a bowling or golf league and strike up conversations with its participants
- Join a business/social group such as Kiwanis International or the Moose Lodge to meet people
- Always carry your business cards to exchange with people you meet. When you meet someone, ask him about himself and what he does. He may be in a business that uses consulting services. Rather than immediately trying to sell your firm, connect with him via LinkedIn or some other social media. If you focus on developing relationships first, the sales process is less forced and more comfortable.

Keeping a network can be beneficial for sales within your firm. It also comes in handy if you find yourself looking for a new job. Contacts have contacts and that's what networking is all about.

Keep in touch with your contacts. Occasionally, go through your network and send an e-mail to three or four contacts to touch base and see how they're doing. When you need to go to them to drum up sales or for help finding a job, they won't view you as one who only contacts them when you need something.

Tip #79: Learn the Client's Business

Case Study:

Ron's first assignment with his new firm was an engagement at the largest banking institution in town. As a business analyst, he would be responsible for learning and documenting an application allowing the bank to collect faster on fees charged for mortgage applications.

He was partnered with Max, who had been with the firm for a few years. Although they were assigned to document requirements for separate components of the application, they attended many meetings that covered overlapping areas.

Ron noticed that Max would often ask questions that applied more to Ron's assigned area than Max's. When Max tried to share requirements from his own areas, Ron wasn't interested. What does that have to do with me, Ron wanted to ask.

After they had been on the project a few weeks, Ron noticed that Max showed interests in other areas outside of his assigned requirements. He wondered if Max had problems focusing. He couldn't figure out why Max seemed so curious about areas of the bank that were unrelated to their project.

One day while they were in the middle of a requirements review, Rita from the client business team was providing details of some business requirements that would affect Ron's assigned work. They wanted some specific mortgage data to be sent to their corporate accounts receivable database.

"That might be a problem," Max interjected.

"Why is that?" Rita asked.

"Well, based on a conversation we had with the mortgage data team, there are privacy rules associated with sharing that data with the AR team."

Ron remembered the conversation, but hadn't made the connection.

"I hadn't even thought of that," Rita replied. "We need to figure out what data we can get and sort that out with them before we define any more requirements. Good catch, Max."

Ron realized that Max's curiosity had given him a broader understanding of their processes, which allowed him to understand obstacles they may run into when communicating with other departments within the bank.

Later that week, the firm's account manager was on-site making her weekly check-in with client management. She always spent an hour with Ron and Max to learn about any issues they had and share any feedback she received from the client.

During that meeting, she asked them how things were going on the project.

"I was in a requirements gathering meeting the other day," Max replied. "During a break, two of the executives began discussing a problem with their mobile checkout app. I asked them a couple of questions to learn a little more about it. It sounds like something our mobile app team could help them with. I thought you ought to know about it."

"That's great Max. I'll look into it," she replied.

A month later, the firm had proposed and won the largest mobile application development project in their history. Max's suggestion had led to it all. At the end of the year, he received public accolades from the firm's president for providing sales leads for three winning projects during the year.

When Ron received his annual performance review one of the suggestions in the areas for improvement was that he take more interest in the client's business functionality outside of his assigned area. He was also told to work harder on identifying possible sales leads.

When assigned to a client site for a project, there is usually a clearly defined scope detailing what will be done to complete the project. In order to be successful, consultants need to understand the client's industry as well as their strategy for success within that industry. Due to time constraints, there is often a tendency to learn only the minimum necessary of the client's business to complete the project successfully.

Motivated consultants dig deeper to gain a thorough understanding of as many details of the client's strategy and business processes as possible. This provides benefits in a number of aspects.

The more you know the client's business, the better your chances of identifying needs for follow-on work.

As follow-on work is identified and won, the client often determines who comes back for another phase. If they see the value in your knowledge of their business, they will specifically request you, insuring higher utilization rates.

Tip #80: Focus on Sales and Billable Hours

To ensure success in consulting, focus on the two areas that most affect the bottom line: sales and billable hours. Billable hours are service hours that can be charged to the client. Internal consulting meetings and other non-client activities can often not be avoided. Any time these situations occur, verify with your management whether it is necessary to attend.

When unassigned to a project you are considered to be on the bench. This is the time to market yourself internally to decision makers within the firm. If a project proposal is being worked on, volunteer to assist. This produces multiple opportunities. You can make yourself known among the decision makers in the firm, potentially get assigned to the project should it be awarded, and possibly receive partial credit for the sale.

While assigned to a project, keen consultants keep their eyes and ears open for new opportunities for add-on sales. While eavesdropping is not recommended, consultants on the front line have the greatest access to identify challenges that their clients have which are outside of the scope of their assigned project. Stumbling across an issue in the normal course of the workday can present opportunities for the firm to do additional work.

It is a generally accepted sales axiom in most industries that it costs more to acquire a new customer than to obtain repeat business from an existing customer. Because of the long sales cycle, this applies more to consulting than in most industries. When new opportunities arise at an existing client, the firm's foot is already in the door. Relationships have already been established and the firm has a known quality factor.

One of the most important factors in this equation is to perform work that the client will value enough to have you back. Identifying sales opportunities while performing poor service will make it difficult to convert to follow-on sales.

Tip #81: Learn from Sales Losses

The sales cycle for most consulting engagements can be long. A client may contact someone they know within the firm and submit a Request for Proposal (RFP). The RFP usually includes a short description of their need for consulting services with various requirements such as the firm's capabilities to do the work, references, and résumés of possible consultants, along with a due date. The firm will usually qualify the company as a viable prospect and then will request time to meet with the client management to learn more about their company, their processes, and the specific request.

After the firm learns more about the candidate client, a proposal team is formed to put together a proposal. This may include a formal Statement of Work (SOW) as well as a PowerPoint presentation highlighting their offering. The proposal may be presented in a bound document and several copies are provided to the candidate.

The proposal usually provides background on the firm including their history, some of their major clients, and their capabilities. Finally, they will present their understanding of the candidate's problem, their proposal for resolving the issue, and the estimated cost of the project, often stated as a dollar range. The process can take several weeks and countless person-hours to bring to completion. The client will usually send RFPs to several firms and select the winning proposal based on pre-defined criteria.

Obviously, not every proposal will be a winner. The client will notify the winning firm and begin negotiations for the project. A representative from each losing firm will then be contacted.

When your firm loses a proposal, ask the client why your firm was not selected. Determine what areas they felt were your strengths and your weaknesses. Their reasons are sometimes specific. Other times, you may learn that their decision was made from the beginning, but they needed three quotes to pass through their finance group. After all of the work to propose, the client owes that much to the losing firms to provide some feedback. Use the feedback--both positive and negative--as lessons learned for future proposals.

Chapter 8 – Career Management

In some industries, moving up the corporate ladder requires doing your job well, playing your politics smartly, not offending the higher-ups, and being loyal to the company. Doing these things well enough will result in the organization managing your career for you.

In consulting, these are just the bare essentials. A consultant is expected to take charge of his own career and be responsible for his own advancement.

Consultants are expected to always be in growth mode and anticipate their next step before they take it. Success occurs when preparation and opportunity intersect. Consultants should be well prepared for opportunities for success, take advantage of the opportunities, and perform at their top level to ensure success for themselves and the firm.

Tip #82: Start Humble, Stay Humble

Firms seek individuals with enough confidence to face tough businesspeople every day and give them advice on how to improve their business. It is not surprising that the manner in which that advice is given is as important as the actual advice.

There is a fine line between advising a client and telling them what to do. Advice is an opinion or recommendation offered as a guide to action. An order is an authoritative direction or instruction. Consultants can assume the expert label and arrogantly tell clients what they should do. A client is more likely to be receptive to advice made as a suggestion backed up by well thought-out logic that shows how it will benefit their organization.

There is a difference between confidence and arrogance. Confidence can be demonstrated modestly, while arrogance is abrasive and condescending.

It's easy to develop a big ego when people see you as the expert. As you progress through your career, you will develop deeper knowledge and a higher confidence level. It is the consultant's responsibility not to let higher levels of knowledge and confidence increase her ego. Don't let your altitude affect your attitude.

Tip #83: Embrace your Failures

As the old baseball saying goes, a liability on the field is an asset on the bench. Or perhaps it's an accounting axiom. Either way, the gist of the saying is that if you screw up you're out of the game.

Unfortunately, many corporate cultures endorse this way of thinking. In an effort to reduce errors, formal and informal policies are put in place to penalize people for making mistakes. Better management would have a higher tolerance for mistakes to encourage risk-taking and a higher level of learning.

Some corporate cultures are more tolerant than others. While a firm may have some tolerance, clients usually have less. Their thinking is usually that the experts were hired for their knowledge and shouldn't be making mistakes. Why should the consultant learn at the client's expense?

There is a famous story from the early days at IBM where an employee made an error that cost the company over $100,000. The employee somberly approached the founder and chairman, Thomas J. Watson, Sr., and said, "I presume, Mr. Watson, that you will expect my resignation."

Watson looked at him and said, "Resignation? I just spent $100,000 training you!"

Although such an enlightened attitude toward screwing up is rare in today's business world, employees should not be afraid to make mistakes. Trying new approaches to problem resolution and taking calculated risks in order to learn better ways to achieve your objectives should be encouraged.

When working several hours per day with tight deadlines and a steady flow of interruptions, it is often difficult to take the time to try multiple approaches to complete a single task. Applying trial and error on a regular basis will usually result in higher learning in a controlled environment that will not expose you or your firm to failure in front of the client.

When blatant mistakes are made in full view of the client, firm management, or both, take full advantage of the situation. Assume responsibility and make amends. Then, take the time to reflect on the following:

- What did you do wrong?
- What could you have done instead?
- What will you do in the future to make sure never to repeat it?

Although an organization may have low tolerance for mistakes, they are much more amendable to them if you acknowledge your mistake and, more importantly, you don't repeat it.

Learning from mistakes should be a group effort. When you see someone else error, try to learn from it. When you make mistakes, share it with your team. That allows them to learn from the mistake, too.

Tip #84: Be a Team Player

Case Study:

Judy and Lisa each led teams on the royalty calculation system for the Wilson Publishing Company. Judy's team had experienced some setbacks and their part of the project was about a week behind. As a result, she asked her team to work longer days to get caught up.

Lisa's team was on schedule and was happy to be working fairly normal hours. At the end of each day, Kerry packed up and left for the day. As Brandon packed up to leave, he asked members of Judy's team if there was anything he could do to help. They explained that the application they were coding was very detailed and had a heavy learning curve. It would take more of their time to bring him up to speed than to complete it themselves, but they thanked Brandon for offering.

At the end of the week, Judy's team had caught up on most of the programming. They were asked to come in over the weekend to test the application. Brandon again offered to come in and help test. Testing the application did not require as much detailed knowledge as programming it and Judy and her team welcomed the additional help.

Brandon sacrificed his Saturday and Sunday to test the application and helped them catch up on the schedule. Judy sent Brandon a formal thank-you message with copies to the project manager and his direct manager.

At the end of the project, Brandon was given a higher score on his evaluation than Kerry. Most importantly, he had established a reputation as a team player within the firm. Brandon was assigned to a high-profile project soon after that. Kerry was on the bench for three weeks until being assigned to an inconsequential project.

Being a team player is a key trait that consulting firms look for and reward in their consultants. Everybody has their own tasks to get done and they need to be responsible for those tasks. The ultimate goal of a project is to get all tasks completed. If you have all of your responsibilities caught up and others on the team are behind, offer help. Sometimes the work is so specialized that additional hands won't help, but there may be other responsibilities, such as administrative tasks, that can be done to help lighten their load.

Helping out your fellow teammates can not only advance your career. Your teammates may just remember what you did the next time you get behind.

Tip #85: Learn from Criticism

Case Study:
Donna had completed her first consulting project. When she went into her performance evaluation she had high expectations. It had been a good experience for her. She felt she had grown and learned much from it. She had gotten along with her project manager and coworkers and received positive feedback from the client.

She met with her project manager, Shannon, who had her performance evaluation in hand. He showed her that she had received a score of three out of a possible five and began to go through each of the evaluation criteria. She was a bit shocked to find out she was just a three, but listened to what he had to say.

Shannon had high praise for her in many aspects. She was an excellent team player and worked well with all of her teammates. She was also willing to work late to get a job done right. Donna scored low in promptness. He told her that there were times when she arrived late for work and that she wasn't always on time for meetings. Donna had a longer commute than the rest of the team and thought that it was okay to get to work a little bit later. She also knew she wasn't at meetings right on time, but they never started on time, so she didn't think it was that big of a deal.

Shannon also told her that he would like her to focus more on details of an issue. There were occasions in client meetings when she was describing an issue where, if they asked for more detail, she would need to follow up with them later. Donna wasn't sure what to say at the end of the meeting. She was glad it was the end of the day. She thanked Shannon and went to her car and cried for fifteen minutes.

That night at home, she reread the performance evaluation several times, wondering if she had failed that badly or if Shannon just didn't like her for some reason. The next morning, she went to his office to talk to him about it. She sat down and asked him what she could have done differently to avoid getting such a poor evaluation.

Shannon was confused. "What makes you think you got a bad evaluation?"

"I think a three out of five is pretty low. You also seemed very critical of my tardiness and attention to detail."

Shannon took a deep breath and began to explain to her. "First of all Donna, when it comes to performance evaluations, we set the bar pretty high. A performance grade of three means you are doing everything we ask you to do. A four means you exceeded almost all of our expectations. Very few people get fours. A five means that you walked on water. Fives are reserved for the few people who are given huge responsibilities and still exceed all of our expectations. Only a couple people in the whole firm get fives.

"This is your first year out of college and your first project. It's nearly impossible to get above a three because you haven't developed your skills enough to exceed any expectations. You also won't get any high-profile opportunities for a while yet.

"As for the criticism, these are minor things, but still things you need to work on. Nobody is perfect. I believe performance reviews should always have some areas to work on, whether they are weaknesses or stretch goals. How else will you continue to grow?"

Donna thought about it and was a little embarrassed. She felt she had overreacted and did not realize that they were valid areas for her to work on to improve herself. In the future, she would be more appreciative and open to suggestions to help her improve.

Consulting requires a thick skin in order to deal with critical and demanding people. A good consultant is always trying to improve and learn and must be able to take criticism and use it as feedback for self-improvement. Criticism is not always constructive. Determine what applies and what doesn't, without being over-sensitive.

Consultants need to have the right balance of leadership, confidence, and intestinal fortitude to properly evaluate criticism. Determine when it is valid for adjustments to be made and when it is simply the client blowing off steam.

Tip #86: Be Flexible

Case Study:

Consulting fitted Carita to a tee. In the past three years, she had been at eight different clients working on ten different projects. She had worked on accounting, inventory management, and claims adjustment applications in industries as varied as banking, manufacturing, and insurance.

Each experience brought on a different challenge with a varied range of personalities. She loved the diversity of experiences that consulting provided. Before she could get bored with a project, she would roll off of that one and move on to the next adventure, usually at another client location.

One Sunday evening as she was watching TV and folding laundry her phone rang. It was Keith, her account manager.

"I'm sorry to bother you on a Sunday evening, but a huge project win just came up over the weekend. Can you be on a plane to New York tomorrow morning?"

"Of course," she replied.

Keith quickly summarized the project and her role on it. He provided her the flight information for the next day. They planned to meet for breakfast at the airport for more details. The next day, the two of them flew to New York and met with the client. At the end of the meeting, she began talking to Patricia, one of the client employees.

"You must have come out here on short notice. I heard they just signed the contract with your firm over the weekend."

"Yes," Carita replied. "Keith called me at home last night."

"And you were able to come out here at a moment's notice?" Patricia asked.

"Yes, it's kind of the nature of consulting," Carita replied. She went on to explain the various experiences she had had going from one client to another, working on different types of systems at every stop.

"And you like that?" Patricia asked, almost incredulously.

"Yes," Carita answered with satisfaction.

After the conversation, Carita thought about Patricia's comment. The thing that Carita loved most about consulting was the very thing that Patricia found undesirable. Carita thought about Patricia's job. She said she had been with her company for about ten years and had been sitting in the same place since day one. She was probably not doing a much different job, very predictable and stable, without many surprises. Carita decided that she probably wouldn't want Patricia's job anymore than Patricia would want hers.

Consulting is not for everybody. It requires the flexibility to work in an unpredictable environment. You can be pulled onto an out-of-town project on short notice. Within a project, tasks change and roles get redefined. As issues arise and skill sets are needed for different tasks or on different projects, consultants are expected to transition quickly from one project to another, handing work off to another member of the team as they move on to the next assignment.

Being flexible does not mean saying yes to every opportunity and request. If you are assigned to a critical project that would be negatively affected by your absence, you will need to weigh the benefits and costs of the proposed move. Most firms will make arrangements with the existing project manager before approaching a consultant about such a change. Some time may be necessary to allow a smooth transition of your responsibilities to someone else. It may require that you spend time on both projects as you ramp up on one while finishing up another.

Tip #87: Stay Abreast of Current Business Trends

Case Study:

As the account manager at her client, Delaney had four different IT projects going in various stages of completion. She met with each project manager every Friday. On Monday she would meet with the client executive for lunch to provide him a consolidated status update.

She always tried to drum up additional business at these lunches, talking about the firm's service offerings and trying to find pain points in his business where her firm could help.

At one of their lunch meetings the client executive asked her about big data. He had been hearing a lot about it lately and wanted to see if it could help his organization be more productive. Delaney had heard about it too. Within her own firm, folks were talking about it in meetings she had attended, but she didn't really know what it was or whether her firm was doing anything with it. She told the client that it was a fairly new concept, but the firm had been discussing it. She promised to follow up with him at the following week's meeting.

Later that week, she met with Carolyn, one of the marketing managers with her firm. She mentioned her client's request. Carolyn told her that the firm had a lot of experience in big data mining and that she would be happy to meet with the client to bring him up to speed on the topic. The next week at the client lunch meeting, she relayed Carolyn's offer of assistance to the client. The client told her that he met with one of her competitors on Tuesday and he filled him in on everything he needed to know. He also stated that her competitor had even discussed his firm's experience with big data and he was more apt to work with them, since they appeared to know it better than her firm.

It is impossible to stay up to date on every industry trend and buzz word. There are usually four to five major trends in any given industry that get a lot of press. Consultants should be aware of the most popular trends and be able to provide a high-level description of each. When a business trend appears to be gaining widespread acceptance, find out if the firm is doing anything to respond to the phenomenon.

There are two aspects from which a consultant should focus.

First, be aware of trends from an industry perspective. Most major industries, such as retail, manufacturing, and pharmaceuticals, have trade journals that discuss the latest trends in their industry. A subscription to a couple of trade magazines will keep one up to date on trends in a specific industry. The *Wall Street Journal* is also an excellent source on general business trends. Additionally, regularly reading blogs on your target industry can be helpful.

The second aspect of awareness should be in your technical specialty. Consulting specialties such as marketing, IT, or strategy often have their own trade journals, blogs, or societies that provide updates on the latest trends.

Tip #88: Adopt Mentors and Accept That They Are not Perfect

Case Study:
After obtaining his MBA, Anton was thrilled to accept a position at a mid-sized strategy consulting firm. He went through a brief orientation and was given the opportunity to work with Don, the branch manager, on three sales proposals that were in progress. Anton was part of a team of three others that produced drafts of the proposals and presented them to Don. Anton marveled at Don's ability to frame questions to the team from the customer's perspective. He gave great suggestions for the content of the proposal and taught the team to familiarize themselves with the firm's service offerings in case a client ever discussed a need that the firm could serve.

As the proposals were completed, the team met with the client prospects to give the sales pitch. Anton became even more impressed with Don as he so eloquently spoke to the client, patiently answering their questions and convincing the clients to use their consulting services. The firm won two of the three projects and Anton was assigned to one of them, a four-person team performing a strategy analysis at a not-for-profit organization.

His project manager, Eric, was an excellent manager. He worked with Anton on honing his presentation skills. There were several evenings where they would stay late in a conference room and Anton would practice giving presentations to Eric. He gave Anton pointers on using speaking aids such as projected images and an easel pad.

Once, in a meeting with the client, the client manager began discussing an issue they had recognized in their market research department. Anton knew that their firm had a practice area that specialized in Business Intelligence. He waited for Eric to bring this up, but he just said he would mention it to Don, the branch manager.

After the meeting he asked Eric why he didn't describe their BI offering to the client.

"Sales just isn't my thing. I hand that all over to Don."

Eric did relay the message to Don later that week. But by the time Don spoke to the client, they were already in talks with another firm that had pounced on the opportunity. Anton was disappointed. Don had taught him to always be prepared to sell. He held Eric on such a pedestal and felt a little let down.

Over time, he learned that both Don and Eric had different skill sets that he valued and could learn from. He continued to learn from each of them. As his career progressed, he met more people with skills that he wanted to develop. He worked closely with them and learned from them. He found that some people had different approaches to doing the same thing and that he could learn from each approach.

Nobody is perfect. Some people make the mistake of choosing one person to be a mentor and hitch their wagon to that star. Everyone has something to teach. Many skills can be learned by keeping your eyes and ears open and observing peoples' approach to various skills. Areas such as sales, public speaking, leadership, and negotiating are great ones to watch. Ask questions.

Some people will be more willing than others to take the time to teach the skills they have learned.

You may not agree with all of the advice you are given. All advice is optional and you should choose which advice works best for you and which to pass up.

As you grow and develop skills, remember how important learning was to you early in your career and take the time to assist consultants younger or less experienced than you.

Tip #89: Get Organized

Case Study:

The status meeting started and everyone sat down at the conference table--everyone except Elizabeth, that is. They began the meeting and at ten minutes after the hour, Elizabeth came rushing in.

"Hi, sorry I'm late," she said. She offered no further explanation.

Her project manager, Helen, was fuming. She noticed a couple of client employees make eye contact and smile. She wondered which one of them won the bet for how many minutes Elizabeth would be late.

After the meeting, Helen stopped by Elizabeth's cubicle. She could barely see any of the desktop from the haystack of papers strewn about the desk. "Elizabeth, I need to talk to you about the status meeting today."

"Yeah, I thought it went well. Sounds like we're right on track."

Helen struggled to keep from rolling her eyes. "Actually, I wanted to talk about your tardiness. You came in ten minutes late."

"Oh, I'm sorry about that. I forgot about the meeting and just happened to see my status report on my desk, which reminded me."

"That's unacceptable, Elizabeth," Helen replied. "Your tardiness to meetings has become habitual. In addition to that, you have missed several deadlines for your work assignments."

Elizabeth began to get defensive. "Well, Helen, I've been working ten-hour days and have even done work on the weekends to keep up. Maybe my workload is just too much."

Prepared for Elizabeth's response, Helen countered, "The hours you have been working is not the issue. You have put in as much time as anyone on the team, maybe more. I think the issue is with how you manage those hours. You're working hard, but I don't think you're working smart."

Elizabeth looked a little insulted and hurt, "Not smart?"

"Elizabeth, I'm not saying that you aren't smart," Helen said. "I just don't think that you're being smart about your time. You seem disorganized. You arrive at meetings late and often don't come prepared. In last week's status meeting, you forgot your status report. A couple of weeks ago, you were facilitating the priorities meeting and printed the agendas for the wrong meeting. Whenever I come to you for any information, you have to get back to me after you dig through the hundreds of files in your "My Documents" directory. But Elizabeth, more importantly, I've gotten complaints from the client that you don't return their phone calls in a timely manner."

Helen stopped to let this sink in. Elizabeth was quiet, but Helen could tell she was frustrated. Helen continued, "Elizabeth, your disorganization is affecting your performance. You don't have a heavier workload than anyone else on the team. You just need to get organized. Do you make a to-do list for everything you need to get done?"

"That's never worked for me. I have so much to do that I don't have time for it."

"Making a to-do list should take no more than ten minutes a day. It will help you to plan your day, remind you of everything you need to do, and help you prioritize so that you focus on the important items first.

The mess on your desk is also a problem. You can't possibly know what is in this pile of papers."

Helen told Elizabeth that she needed to get organized or she would take her off the project. They worked out an organization plan and Helen met with Elizabeth daily to review her to-do list and to help her stay in the habit of getting organized. After a few weeks, Elizabeth began to see the benefits of being organized. She found that she was working fewer hours and getting more done. She also was arriving to meetings on time.

It is imperative for consultants to be organized. In addition to making them more productive, being organized demonstrates an image of professionalism to the client. In order to be organized:

Each day before you leave, create a to-do list for the next day. This can be done on paper or electronically using Word, Excel, or a calendaring application such as Outlook. List all meetings scheduled for the day and program your calendaring application to provide a five- or ten-minute reminder for each meeting.

Prioritize each task. Examples are:

- A – Tasks that must be completed by the end of the day
- B – Important tasks
- C – Nice-to-have tasks that can be done if time permits.

Organize your files. Rather than keeping every electronic file in one directory, create meaningful directories and be diligent about storing documents in their proper folder.

Organize the papers on your desk. Develop a filing system similar to that of your electronic files. Make sure you file papers in their appropriate folders for easy access. If you need papers at your fingertips, a few neat stacks of paper, organized by function, will be easier to manage and you'll be able to find what you are looking for.

Prepare for meetings in advance. Determine what you need to bring to a meeting and have whatever copies you need printed and ready at least one hour prior to the start of the meeting.

Be disciplined at staying organized. It requires time and effort, but pays for itself many times over.

Tip #90: Talk to a Manager Before Leaving the Firm

In consulting, the pay is above average. You get opportunities that many of your peers working for your clients rarely get. For most people, it's more interesting than what your client peers are doing. The downside, however, is that it can be frustrating. Consulting firms try to hire smart people with excellent communication and leadership skills. They want people with a thick skin that can go toe-to-toe with clients and will go the extra mile to get a job done on time within budget. Consultants stay late until the work is done, while the client employees make a beeline for the door at 4:30 PM every day. When the project is finished, the client employees take credit for everything that went right and blame the consultants for everything that went wrong. On top of all of that, there seems to be one person at each client who gets his or her thrills abusing consultants, reminding them of the rates they are paying every chance they get.

Staying too long at one client under difficult circumstances can begin to wear on even the strongest consultant. A change of pace is often in order, even if it is just to get a new group of people to be abused by. The consultant may start to feel that management at the firm doesn't care about the pressure he is under. They keep their mouths shut and try to tough it out. There are many other reasons in which a consultant can become unhappy. Eventually, they begin testing the job market and, assuming a decent hiring market and their experience at the firm provided them with marketable skills, they find another job.

261

Unfortunately, it most likely won't be any better at another firm. All firms have clients and all client projects have pressure. Leaving consulting may be the answer if you decide that consulting isn't for you--and it isn't for everyone. But while the work in an industry job may have lower stress and shorter hours, the work may be less challenging and interesting.

Depending on the circumstances, leaving consulting or leaving your firm may turn out to be the best answer. Before making that leap, however, it is in your best interest and that of the firm to sit down with management and explain why you are unhappy. Consultants are often afraid to complain for fear that management will label them a whiner who can't handle the pressure. That is a valid concern, but if you are considering leaving the firm anyway, what have you got to lose?

Before surprising your firm with a resignation, sit down with a manager to discuss your situation:

- Talk to her about facts rather than emotional terms. You may be burnt out, frustrated, and depressed, but she will be much more receptive to your issues if you talk about the number of hours you have worked and the results you have achieved before discussing feeling like you need a change of pace.
- Make it clear to your manager that you like working for the firm and enjoy the work. She needs to know that your frustration is with the client and not the firm or consulting in general. If she thinks you will be just as unhappy at another client, she will be reluctant to make a move.
- If there is one person that is being unnecessarily abusive, particularly if it is sexual or discriminatory, firm management may be able to talk to the client

about the person. If no laws are being broken and the person is just a jerk, your manager should be made aware, but may not be able to have any effect with client management, depending on the person's level within the client.

The firm may not have any immediate options at the time you talk with them. There may be no other projects that fit your skills or they may need you to finish the project you are on. You will need to decide whether you can continue or need to make a job change early.

Tip #91: Learn to Summarize

Case Study:

Tuesday was status day on Caty's project. As project manager, she held a status meeting every Tuesday morning at 9:00 with her team of two business analysts and seven programmers. Caty tried to make the meeting as efficient as possible. She had been through far too many status meetings where managers went around the room soliciting input that had no value to the others present. She knew that wasn't the most effective use of everyone's time. Caty felt the status meeting should be a forum to discuss issues that could affect others on their productivity and to share ideas that were of value to the rest of the team. She also knew that every minute the team was in a meeting was a lost minute of productivity.

Ralph was one of the programmers on her team. He was an excellent programmer who was detail oriented and produced high-quality work. When he brought up issues in the status meetings, he often liked to share every detail of his code logic with the full team in order to get to the point of the issue. Caty had seen him speak for ten minutes once in a meeting, explaining in great detail several scenarios on how financial transactions were matched and processed before getting to the point of his issue. Caty had spoken to him a number of times about being too verbose and trying to develop more abridged descriptions, but Ralph's response was, "I don't know how to do it any other way."

Good managers want summaries of issues with just enough detail to help them make a decision on resolution. Providing every detail of an issue often wastes the whole team's time and causes them to become impatient. If every employee provided such minute detail for every issue, managers wouldn't have time to do their jobs. This applies when presenting issues and task summaries to client management as well.

Some managers do request as much detail as possible. There are times when they need more detail in order to make a decision. It is important to have the detailed information available in case they need it.

The best approach is to start out with a high-level overview and begin drilling down. As you get to the level of detail with which they are comfortable enough to make a decision, stop. Let them know if there are additional details that should be known before a decision is made, but make certain they are pertinent to the decision.

Tip #92: Provide Options When Presenting an Issue

Case Study:
Enid identified an issue regarding the mapping of data from the legacy software system to the new application. She went to Carlos, her project manager, to discuss the issue. She explained the details of the problem and asked him what to do.

"What do you think are the best options?" he asked her.

"I'm not sure," she responded. "What do you think?"

"You're the consultant, Enid. I want you to go back and think about it. List out the best three options and try to determine the best alternative. If you have trouble deciding, bring those options to me with the pros and cons for each and I'll try to help you decide."

Enid walked away frustrated. She knew Carlos was just making it difficult on her. She went to her desk and stared at the wall. Finally, she pulled out a pad of paper and began drawing diagrams of the data mapping and alternate options. She came up with some ideas, but none of them seemed like the perfect solution.

After she came up with several options, she took the three that she thought were best and went back to Carlos. They discussed each option along with the advantages and disadvantages of each. Finally Carlos suggested a tweak to one of her options. As they diagrammed it out, it proved to be the optimal solution.

Enid realized that Carlos could have worked the solution out himself, given enough time, but it was her job to attempt to resolve the problem herself. If she was not able to resolve it completely, at least her work would give him a head start so he wouldn't have to spend so much time on it.

A consultant's job is to be a problem solver. It takes a combination of creativity and analytical skill to identify a solution. When issues are identified you must try to identify the best solution to the issue. If the issue is complex, identify as many possible resolutions as you can. List the pros and cons to each resolution. It is acceptable to solicit help from a manager, peer, or someone with adequate knowledge to provide input, but always have some potential solutions for him to consider. It will assist him in the brainstorming process and will show that you have thought out the process and made an attempt to solve the problem yourself.

This is most important when addressing issues to the client--they look to you for solutions, not problems.

Tip #93: Focus on Solutions, Not Blame

Case Study:

The implementation of the distribution software system had gone south and things were not improving. Deadlines had been missed for three weeks straight and were continuing to slip.

Computer servers that had been ordered from a low-cost provider had been placed on back-order. They were critical dependencies for the software installation. As a result, testing would also be delayed.

Nan, the account manager, had been getting weekly updates on the delays, but as word of the hardware holdup came she decided to catch the next flight out and meet with the team. Nan met with the project manager and each of the team leads at 8:00 the next morning.

The team settled into the conference room and she began the meeting. "This project has gotten a little off track and we need to decide in this meeting what needs to be done to get it back on track. It needs to start moving toward completion."

Mike was the first to speak up. "We should never have purchased the hardware from that cut-rate joint. If Jon hadn't been such a cheapskate, we wouldn't be sitting here."

Matt, the project manager, chimed in. "The estimates totally sucked as well. We've been working under such unrealistic expectations that it's ridiculous. I knew it would put us behind. Julie crammed these estimates down our throats and then went on to her next assignment. She should be in this meeting to face the music."

Nan stopped them right there. "The purpose of this meeting is not to have anyone face any music. We can sort out who did what later in a lessons-learned session. Right now, we need to determine what is wrong and find viable solutions to correct it and get the project right again."

For the next two hours they listed all of the delays of the project to date and what it would take to get each task completed. They updated the project plan with realistic estimates for each task and added time for the hardware delay. They determined that the team would need to put in some longer days and they would add two more people to the team. For an additional fee, they could expedite delivery of the servers.

In the end, the project deadline needed to be pushed out by three weeks and their budget would need to increase to accommodate the extra team members and the expediting fee. This would be difficult to explain to the client and to the firm's management, but it was a realistic plan that showed they were willing to dedicate the resources to get the job done.

On any complex project, despite the best-laid plans, things are bound to go wrong. People make mistakes; deadlines get missed. When this happens, there is a tendency to get defensive and find someone to blame. Some people react by getting angry, yelling at people or throwing things. None of these reactions do anything to solve the problem.

When things go wrong, there are times when it is appropriate to discipline people if they are ineffective or neglectful. The main focus should be on how to correct the situation and move forward. Crying over spilled milk doesn't clean up the mess.

Tip #94: Focus on the Right Measurement Metrics

Case Study:

"Now that you're a senior manager, you'll be responsible for more business development. In fact, forty percent of your evaluation criteria will be based on whether you make your sales numbers," Gene explained to Heidi.

Heidi had just been informed by her boss of her promotion to senior manager. This was a big step for her. She was now just one step away from partner. That would take a few more years, but Heidi was willing to do whatever it took to make partner.

She had been working on her networking skills most of her career. Getting involved in sales proposals over the past few years as a manager had been enlightening, also. As a senior manager, she would be responsible for identifying leads and leading proposal teams to win projects for the firm.

Over the next year, she did just that. She aggressively contacted people from her network and talked to them about their consulting needs. In addition to her billable work to her clients, she led seven proposal teams trying to sell large-scale projects. Four of the projects successfully sold. Unfortunately, they were projects for services that her firm had little experience in. Moreover, they had never worked in the industries for these clients.

During execution of those projects, the teams suffered. There were no subject matter experts. They often had to search the Internet to stay a step ahead of the client.

The teams were required to work longer days to catch up on their knowledge. Morale suffered along with client satisfaction. They managed to limp over the finish lines of each project. Despite attempts by the firm to sell follow-on work, the clients opted not to do business with them anymore.

Because Heidi sold four major delivery projects in her first year as a senior manager, she received public accolades and awards from the executive team, including a large bonus. Based on the sales numbers she was measured by, she was a big success.

It starts at an early age. Teachers and parents tell us that to be successful and smart we have to get good grades. Their intentions are good. They assume that if you get a good grade in a class, that you studied hard and learned the material. But some students figure out that you don't have to study. You can copy from your neighbor, steal the test scores, or find some other creative way to get the grade if that's all you want.

Some kids are given an allowance if they keep their rooms clean. If the parent doesn't check the closet, under the bed, or the hamper full of clean clothes, the allowance is easily earned.

Throughout life, we're given incentives that are intended to encourage a certain behavior. Make your numbers and get rewarded.

Consulting firms create incentives to influence desired behaviors. Early in one's consulting career a consultant is motivated toward high utilization. Getting assigned to billable projects and staying billable keeps the revenue coming in the door. But some consultants learn that they can pad their time sheets to increase their utilization.

As the consultant moves up the career ladder, the incentive for utilization decreases and is gradually replaced by incentives to sell.

Sales incentives often encourage anyone trying to sell services to just go out and sell. It doesn't matter whether we know how to do it. Just sell it and we'll get some training or learn it as we go. Maybe we'll hire an expert on it to help us out until we come up to speed.

This is a thorny route to becoming a trusted advisor to your clients. The firm is essentially using the client and billing them for the time it takes them to learn.

The firm's goal should be long-term relationships to become the client's trusted advisor. Selling one large project in an area where the firm lacks expertise may limit the relationship to that single project.

If the firm helps the client find a more appropriate firm to implement the project, it may hurt their revenues in the short run--along with helping a potential competitor. But it will better position the firm as the client's trusted advisor, resulting in a long-term relationship that can lead to many more engagements in the future.

Regardless of the firm's incentive structure, individual consultants should focus their sales efforts on what is best for their clients. Finding a new client is much more expensive than keeping an existing one. Maintaining a concentration on the long-term relationship will result in better sales numbers for the individual consultant as well as for the firm.

Tip #95: Be Prepared for Long Days

Case Study:

As a child growing up, Lee remembered his father coming home from work at 5:30 every night like clockwork. His father would change clothes and his mother would have dinner ready by 5:45.

When Lee graduated from college, he took a job at an insurance company in a nearby city and followed a similar schedule as his father. He would finish work at 5:00 PM and arrive home about 5:30. After about five years in the insurance industry, he had developed some in-depth knowledge of the industry. Recruiters began calling him suggesting that he consider a career in consulting. The pay was much better and his expertise in the insurance industry would be in high demand with consulting firms.

After careful consideration and a lot of discussion with his wife, Lee decided to take the plunge. He interviewed with several consulting firms and accepted an offer with a local firm.

His first couple of weeks consisted of orientation and what he came to know as bench time. Finally, in his third week, he was assigned to a client located an hour and fifteen minutes away from his house. This was a four-month assignment and he felt he could deal with the long commute for a temporary period.

Once at the client site, Lee spent several days assisting the project manager on start-up activities. They would stay until 6:00 or 6:30 PM, well after the client's employees left for the day. As the project progressed, quitting time varied based on what needed to get done and how many road blocks they ran into during the day.

275

Lee noted that nobody on the project team left until all of the planned tasks for the day were completed.

The last month of the project came and they were approaching "crunch time." The deadline loomed in the near future. They were going through the testing phase and were putting in even longer days. Sometimes Lee didn't get out of the office until 9:00 or 10:00 PM. He realized that the time flew. The work was so much more interesting and it was fun working as a team to accomplish a major goal. He would leave the office exhausted and invigorated at the same time. In the morning, he would immediately begin thinking of his to-do list for the day and the many things he wanted to get done.

The project finished on time and within budget. The project manager took the team out for celebratory drinks where they all patted themselves on the back for a job well done. A few days later, they learned that the firm had won a follow-on project at the client and, because of his hard work and expertise, Lee would be playing a critical role on the project team. Lee was prepared to do it all over again.

Most consulting firms will contend that they hire the best and the brightest. For the most part, that is true. Top tier firms select students with high GPAs from the top-ranked schools. They then screen that group to find the ones they think have the most initiative that will succeed in the high-powered, high-stressed consulting environment.

An additional criteria that firms look for is someone who is hard working and not afraid to work overtime to get the job done. Client employees generally work a standard eight-hour workday. As much as consultants would like to believe in their superiority over client staff in their effectiveness and intelligence, the key reason they get more done than the client is that they simply put in longer hours.

Additionally, many projects are performed in conjunction with an offshore team in a country such as India or China. Since they work on the opposite side of the clock, conference calls are often scheduled for late in the night in the United States, which is early in the morning for the offshore team.

Most firms, in general, don't require extraordinarily long days on a permanent or long-term basis, but consultants are expected to work long days when a deadline requires it. This can come at the spur of the moment, when a problem occurs that needs to be resolved to avoid a schedule delay. It also occurs as the deadline of a project approaches and there is little time left to make up for delays. At this time, usually the last four to six weeks of a project, evening and weekend work is not unusual. While client employees may be headed for the door when their workday ends, the consultants stay and get the work done to make sure the project completes at its scheduled time.

Ironically, this is part of what makes consulting enjoyable for many. Working hard in a team environment to accomplish a difficult task is its own reward. When it's all over and done with, the pleasure was worth all the pain.

Tip #96: Promotions Come When You Begin Performing at the Next Level

Case Study A:
Marlin had been with his firm for over two years. In that time, he had paid close attention to his job description and performance evaluation criteria. He felt he had done everything they had asked of him and, as the end-of-year promotions were about to be announced, he anticipated being promoted to consulting senior. He entered his performance evaluation with the regional manager with high hopes. The RM gave Marlin high marks and high praise. At the end of the conversation, he told him that he would get a raise, but there was no mention of a promotion. When Marlin ask about a promotion, the RM said that he had done well this year and had even exceeded their expectations in certain areas, but that he hadn't performed to the level that would give them reason to promote him.

Case Study B:
Sandra started with the firm the same week as Marlin. Over the past two years, she had sought out additional responsibilities on each of her projects. While on client sites, she developed relationships with key client personnel and identified issues that led to potential new work at the client. At the quarterly internal meeting, she volunteered to give part of the presentation that showcased their successful project to the rest of the firm. When Sandra met with the regional manager for her performance review, he gave her much of the same high praise that was given to Marlin. He also told her that she was being promoted to consulting senior. At this new level, she would be expected to identify new project

opportunities and take on new responsibilities. He was certain that she would be successful in this role because she had already begun doing many of the responsibilities.

Many of the higher-level consulting firms have an informal "up-or-out" policy. If you are not consistently moving up the organizational ladder, you will soon be moved out.

Client firms allow employees to meet their expectations on a year-to-year basis. Consulting firms want to see growth and ambition in their employees. Simply doing everything that is expected of you will rarely result in a promotion. Advancing up the ladder usually occurs when a consultant proves that she has the skills, confidence, and determination to begin working at the next level before the title is given to her.

Tip #97: Working from Home Is not a Day Off

Case Study:

As a cost-cutting effort, Spencer's firm reduced their downtown office space significantly. They maintained just enough space to allow internal projects to be executed. Eighty-five percent of their employees were delegated to work-from-home status. Each employee had his or her own laptop and was given an allowance for a printer, paper, and other supplies needed for a home office. Spencer was on the bench and loved this set up.

He had to be on periodic conference calls--bench calls--for anyone not assigned to a project. In these calls, management would attempt to assign team members to any proposals or internal projects being worked on. Spencer got the occasional assignment and worked on it in his spare time. He was much more interested in watching *Sports Center* and getting personal errands done. As a result, his assignments were handed in later and with lower quality than his manager expected.

After about two weeks, his manager called him to discuss what she had been noticing. She expressed her concerns about the quality and timeliness of his assignments and asked if he was putting one hundred percent into his work when he was at home. Spencer knew he was busted and promised to make things right.

Working from home is a practice that is gaining popularity. The economic downturn has motivated all businesses to pursue cost-cutting programs. Allowing employees to work from home allows them to significantly reduce overhead costs if they can reduce their office space. This is a considerable leap of faith for some managers who are concerned that workers will not be motivated to work as hard as they normally would on-site--away from a manager's watchful eye. Some firms accept that if there is nothing to assign to the worker it is okay. The long hours on previous projects justify getting some free time on the firm. Other firms want to leverage the slack time for work on proposals or internal projects to improve their processes for future projects. If your firm allows work-from-home arrangements:

- Make sure to let management know that you are available and willing to work on whatever needs to be done. Volunteer for work that you happen to be aware of, especially proposal work. This is non-billable work that you can still get credit for if the proposal results in a project. It also increases your chance of being assigned to the project.

- Make your schedule available to your manager. Let them know when you are on conference calls and enter tasks you are working on through the day in your calendar to let them know you *are* working.

- Always be available by phone and e-mail. When managers try texting, calling, and e-mailing with no response, they begin to wonder what you are up to.

- If you need to be away to run a personal errand or will be unavailable for any reason, let your manager know.

- Avoid sending unnecessary e-mails every couple of hours simply to let people know that you are working. It is usually transparent and could make them wonder what you might be covering up.

Tip #98: Optimize Your Bench Time

Consulting firms measure their employees' performance in many aspects, but the two most important measurement metrics for consultants are their utilization (hours billed to clients) and their sales numbers.

Sales numbers can be awarded to consultants as a percentage of a project's value by assisting on a winning proposal, identifying a client need for which new work resulted, or sometimes by providing work at such a high quality level the client asked for add-on work. Firms often utilize benched employees for internal projects-- jobs that they do to create internal tools or processes to improve their own productivity, such as development of a knowledge base. When you are on the bench:

- Seek out sales proposals that are currently being worked on. Ask if there is any assistance needed on any proposal teams. Even mundane tasks like running copies or proofreading can provide exposure and get a foot in the door for more significant work. It also shows management that you are willing to do whatever it takes to help them get sales.
- In larger firms, it may be necessary to do some internal schmoozing with management. Let them know your skill set and that you are available for new projects and proposals.

Some consultants follow a strategy of keeping a low profile when less-desirable work, such as an internal project, is being staffed. They feel it is better for their career in the long run to be on higher-profile client projects. It is true that billable projects are held in higher esteem, but laying low can result in missed opportunities also. It is better to show management a consistent willingness to do what it takes to get a job done, regardless of the job. That attitude and work ethic is more likely to get a consultant assigned to a high-profile job when the opportunity arises.

Tip #99: Protect the Firm's Confidential Information

Case Study:

The six-month implementation of the accounting system at Buchanan Distribution Services was winding down. Cameron had done an excellent job as project manager. It was going to be finished on time and well under budget. The client was pleased. Cameron's firm was pleased. This was their first project with Buchanan and they were hoping to acquire a lot more business from them.

It was a competitive environment. Buchanan had several consulting firms on-site running various projects. Consultants were scattered about all over the company's headquarters building. It was sometimes hard to differentiate between the employees and the consultants.

Cameron was working on the proposal for a new project that his firm was bidding on with Buchanan. It was a much more significant project involving a larger team for a longer duration. For their current project, Cameron's firm had reduced their margin significantly to get their foot in the door at Buchanan. Now that they had proven their capabilities, they were planning to bid for a higher profit margin.

Cameron finished the proposal and printed it to review it. The proposal document was thirty-two pages long and provided all the detail of their approach to the project, including details of their methodology, the number of people they would staff on the project, and their pricing. He also printed the pricing model. The pricing model was a proprietary tool of the firm which would calculate their margin based on each consultant's billing rate and cost. It also factored in travel, per diem expenses and other costs to give them their true profit margin for the proposed project.

He sat down to review the documents and his mobile phone rang. His boss wanted an update on the current project. Cameron stepped into a nearby conference room to avoid disturbing others in the area. He spent about fifteen minutes updating his boss and answering his questions. When he returned to his desk the printed proposal and pricing model couldn't be found. He scoured the desk and the floor around it. He even went back to the conference room to see if he had carried it with him while he spoke to his boss. He finally gave up looking and printed new copies.

The next week, his firm presented their proposal. The executives at Buchanan Distribution Services seemed receptive to their approach and Cameron thought the presentation went well. They were told that they had three other firms to meet with and would have a decision by the end of the week.

Cameron received a call on Friday from Tammy Sanderson, the director of IT at Buchanan. She told Cameron that they had decided to go with another firm. This firm had a very similar approach and methodology as Cameron's firm, but they had priced it significantly lower. Cameron recognized the competing firm's name. They had consultants that sat near his desk at Buchanan.

All organizations have proprietary and confidential information that needs to be protected. Employees need to be aware when they are in possession of such confidential information and take steps to protect it.

Confidential papers should never be left out in the open for clients or competitors to see. If the client provides a desk that locks, papers should be locked in a desk drawer when you step away. Data on a computer is just as important. Computers should be locked by password when you are away from your desk. When using a laptop, it should be either physically locked down to the desk, or carried with you wherever you go. When carrying a laptop in your car, it's best to keep it in the trunk or stored somewhere that it cannot be seen.

In addition to keeping confidential firm information away from the eyes of competitors, clients should not be privy to proprietary firm information. Profit margin, consultant salaries, and work being done for other clients should not be revealed to the client. Their focus should be steered toward the value they receive for consulting services in return for their fees rather than how much the firm is earning in fees.

Tip #100: Think Twice Before Refusing a Project

Case Study:
Having finished a nine-month out-of-town project, Jonathan needed some time to recharge his batteries. Back at his Atlanta office, he spent a week archiving project artifacts to the knowledge repository and completing the final project close-down activities. Once he completed those tasks, he sniffed around for any proposals that were being worked on. The few that were active were in their final stages so he went on work-from-home status to wait for his next assignment.

Jessica, his account manager, called him after a few days and said she had a project that would be right up his alley. They needed someone with his qualifications on a three-month assignment in Philadelphia.

"Philadelphia?" he asked. "Aren't there any projects locally?"

"None that fit your skill set," Jessica answered.

"Are there any in the pipeline?"

"A few, but nothing definite," Jessica replied.

Jonathan was a little road weary from the past nine months and was not too crazy about spending a winter in Philadelphia. "I think I'll pass on this project and wait to see what pulls through the pipeline," he finally said.

Jessica was a little surprised by his response. "I really think you should take this opportunity, Jonathan. There is no guarantee that anything will hit locally any time soon."

"I'll take my chances," said Jonathan confidently.

After hanging up, Jessica relayed the conversation to Jay, the regional manager. Jay called Jonathan and told him to be on a plane to Philly on Monday.

Jonathan did as he was told and served on the Philadelphia project for four months before rolling off. After that, he realized that his peers seemed to get better opportunities on higher profile projects than he did. When he met with Jay for his annual performance evaluation, his numbers were lower than usual as were his raise and bonus.

It's rare to be given a choice on project assignments, especially at the lower-level ranks within a consulting firm. Great opportunities and projects that don't include travel may coincide with times that you are available… and they may not.

It is common to find out that you will roll off of a project in the final week. Other times you may be given longer notice. As soon as you find out even an approximate project roll-off date:

- Notify the person in charge of project staffing to let them know when you will be available. Even if they have your skills inventory, update them with any new skills that you may have developed on your current project.
- At this time, it is appropriate to tell them what type of work you would like to do, including your travel preference. This should be stated as a request rather than a demand.
- If they ask you if you are willing to do something that you do not want to do--such as travel--tell them that you would rather not if there was another option, but avoid using terms such as "unwilling."

Personal considerations such as work-life balance need to be evaluated. If the firm clearly stated that there would be travel involved and it conflicts with your family commitments you may need to turn down a project. You may want to consider using the extra time to update your résumé and begin looking for another job.

A reputable firm that values retaining good employees will do whatever they can to accommodate your needs. If you feel you want a certain opportunity to grow in your career or need to take a break from travel, you should express your concerns to your manager. Her response could range from, "That's just the way it is here, only the strong survive," to, "I'll try to get you assigned to something more suitable for you." Either way, you will know where you stand and you will have expressed your needs to management. If you decide to leave the firm, it will not be a total surprise to them.

Firms want to accommodate their valuable consultants' needs for the most part. You must keep in mind that as hard as they may try to accommodate your needs, the opportunities may not come up at the same times as you are available. It is subject to the luck of the draw. If you take the less-desirable projects when they come, a good firm will take note of it and try to make it up to you on the next assignment.

Tip #101: Have a Passion for What You Do

Consulting can be a demanding profession. Despite the challenges, it can also be rewarding. Like any occupation, it has to be a good fit for the individual's personality and work ethic. Consulting is not a good fit for people who want a standard nine-to-five work schedule and like to work in a predictable environment. However, if you like:

- Having a different challenge every day
- Thinking creatively to solve complex problems
- Being given leadership opportunities on a regular basis
- Living in a frequently chaotic state
- Brainstorming ideas and facilitating a group to agreement on a solution
- Driving yourself and others to complete an accomplishment by a designated time
- Working with people of different cultures, priorities, and personalities
- Feeling a sense of accomplishment when you've given everything you have--emptied your tank--to complete a project successfully,

...then perhaps consulting is for you.

If your heart is not in your work, success is unlikely. It is important that you have a passion for what you do. When Steven Spielberg was filming *Raiders of the Lost Ark* in 1981, he was quoted as turning to George Lucas and saying, "Can you believe people pay us to do this?" He had a passion for what he did and loved it so much he would have done it for no pay.

Perhaps doing it for no pay is a little extreme, but if you feel that you are the person described above, I encourage you to jump in with both feet and give it

100%. You have the tools to be successful, now you just need to provide the passion.

Afterward

Throughout this book it may appear that I have painted a picture of consulting as a high-stress, politically charged occupation in which long hours are the norm and where a single screw-up will get you booted from a client site. Take solace that this stormy picture points out the worst-case scenarios to show the reader what not to do. Many of these examples have come from real-life situations and are meant to be lessons learned in an effort to avoid making the same mistakes.

What I may have been remiss in including in this portrait are the many advantages and benefits that a career in consulting offers:

- Consultants are often given more interesting assignments that clients may not offer to their own employees. When a client firm has a critical, high-profile project to complete, they usually feel safer bringing in a team of experts rather than risking it on their own employees. It is often the case that client employees do day-to-day maintenance work while consultants are brought in to solve problems.
- Consultants often receive more training than a client employee. Because consulting firms need to stay ahead of the curve in the latest technologies, business practices, and trends, they generally provide their employees more advanced training and higher level experience. That makes them more marketable throughout their career.

- Consulting projects are typically structured around teams and camaraderie is built among the team members. This results in stronger working relationships.
- By working in teams and always striving as a team toward a common goal, there is a greater sense of accomplishment when finishing a project together.
- Although consultants can work on a series of projects with the same client, they most commonly work a project for six to twelve months and move on to another project at another client. This allows the individual to work in a diversity of settings, never getting bored of the same surroundings year after year.
- Finally, consulting generally pays better than standard client employment. Consultants are expected to take on added responsibilities and are usually compensated accordingly.

Thank you for reading. Please provide a review for this book on the site at which you purchased it.

Order Lew's other books today:

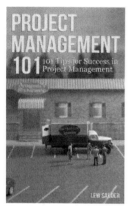

Project Management 101: 101 Tips for Success in Project Management

The Reluctant Mentor: How Baby Boomers and Millenials Can Mentor Each Other in the Modern Workplace

Glossary of Consulting Terms

Billing Rate: Amount charged to the client for consulting work. Usually stated as a per-hour rate, but also can be daily, weekly, or some other agreed-upon measure.

Blended Rate: Average rate of all workers at all levels. This allows the firm to provide an average cost per hour without revealing the actual rates of each worker at each level.

Business Process Re-engineering (BPR): A process where the current workflows of an organization are analyzed and redesigned for greater efficiency.

Client Site: Consulting customer's office location.

Contingency: Risk-management tool used when estimating a project; the addition of hours to a project budget allowing for unknowns that will increase the time and/or cost of a project.

Decision Maker: Client executive(s) responsible for choosing a consulting firm for a project.

Deliverable: Something provided to a client as the product of development, usually documentation or a software application.

Face-time: Time spent on a client site, visible by the client.

Fixed-Bid Contract: Contract that stipulates a price which is not subject to change unless certain conditions are included in the agreement; usually negotiated when requirements are well known. Also called Fixed-Price Contract.

Gantt Chart: Bar-type chart that displays a project schedule by illustrating the start and finish dates of the summary and task elements of a project.

Gap Analysis: Business analysis tool that helps a company compare its current workflow with potential (or future state) workflow to determine the changes needed to get from one point to another.

Go Live: Date in which a planned system will be deployed to production for all intended users to access.

Implementation: Execution of a project in which a product is left behind for the client's use.

Master Services Agreement (MSA): Legally binding contract between a consulting firm and their client detailing responsibilities and obligations of each party.

Methodology: Practices, procedures, and standards used by a consulting firm to create a consistent approach to service delivery across all clients and projects.

Offshoring: Transferring a business function to another country, usually to reduce the costs.

On the Bench: The status of a consultant who is not assigned to a billable project. Also called "On the beach."

Outsource: Subcontracting work to another firm or individual.

Per Diem (Latin for *per day*): Daily allowance for expenses while traveling. Some clients prefer to pay a set amount rather than allow the consultant unlimited budget for expenses.

Project Charter: Project document created at the beginning of a project that defines a project's scope, objectives, main stakeholders, roles and responsibilities, and project objectives.

Project Sponsor: Client manager that is ultimately responsible for the project's success.

Proposal: Consulting sales tool written to convince a client to contract with the firm. Usually a formal document given with a presentation that states, in exchange for consulting fees, the firm will provide services (analysis of a procedure, tax advice, software application) or do something the client wishes to have done.

Request for Proposal (RFP): An invitation from a business for service providers to bid on the right to supply a service.

Sales Pipeline: Sales prospects at different points in the sales cycle, varying from leads to those ready to close.

Scope: Definition of the work that needs to be accomplished to deliver a project with the specified features and functions.

Scope Creep: Uncontrolled changes that add additional, unplanned work to a project.

Statement of Work (SOW): Detailed description of the specific services a consultant will perform under contract.

Steering Committee: A group of executive stakeholders whose role is to provide governance on overall project direction.

Subject Matter Expert (SME): Individual with specialty knowledge of a business process or area designated to provide input and answer questions on a project.

Timebox: Time management practice of setting a specific time limit for an activity. The activity is stopped, regardless of its status once the set time has elapsed.

Time & Materials Contract (T&M): Contract in which a consulting firm is paid on the basis of actual cost, usually at specified hourly rates.

Utilization: Billable hours worked for a client, usually expressed in a percentage. If a consultant worked forty hours in a week, and billed ten, her utilization would be twenty-five percent.

Value Proposition: The positive worth a consulting firm offers to its client to induce them to purchase their services.

Vendor: In a business to business (B2B) environment, a firm that provides products or services to another company.

About the Author

Lew Sauder has worked in consulting with top-tier and boutique firms for over twenty years. He has also served as an IT Manager outside of consulting as a client manager for five years in which he has sat on the other side of the desk, hiring and managing consulting firms.

Lew has a BS in Applied Computer Science from Illinois State University and an MBA from Northwestern University's Kellogg School of Business. He is a certified Project Management Professional (PMP) with the Project Management Institute

He lives in the Chicago suburbs with his wife and family.